CORE STABILITY

injury free performance

CORE STABILITY
injury free performance

Reprinted 2007

A CIP catalogue record for this book is available from the British Library.

Printed by: PLP Commercial Printers Ltd
Impressions House, 3-7 Mowlem Street, London E2 9HE

Published by P2P Publishing Ltd

P2P Publishing Ltd is a trading name of Electric Word plc
Registered office: 33-41 Dallington Street, London, EC1V 0BB
Tel: 0845 450 6402
Registered number: 3934419

ISBN: 978-1-905096-22-4

Publisher Jonathan A. Pye
Editor Jane Taylor
Designer The Flying Fish Studios Ltd

OTHER TITLES IN THE PEAK PERFORMANCE SPECIAL REPORT SERIES

ACHILLES TENDINITIS – PREVENTION AND TREATMENT

CARBO LOADING – FOR THAT EXTRA EDGE

COACHING YOUNG ATHLETES

CREATINE – CUTTING THROUGH THE MYTHS

DYNAMIC STRENGTH TRAINING FOR SWIMMERS

TRAINING FOR MASTER ATHLETES

FEMALE ATHLETES – TRAINING FOR SUCCESS

SHOULDER INJURIES – PREVENTION AND TREATMENT

MARATHON TRAINING – FOR YOUR PERSONAL BEST

NUTRITIONAL SUPPLEMENTS – BOOSTING YOUR PERFORMANCE

SPORTS PSYCHOLOGY – THE WILL TO WIN

TRAINING FOR SPEED, POWER & STRENGTH

ALL WEATHER TRAINING – BEATING THE ELEMENTS

BODY FUEL – FOOD FOR SPORT

TRAINING FOR ENDURANCE

FOOTBALL PERFORMANCE – HOW TO RAISE YOUR GAME

TRAINING FOR RUGBY

TRAINING FOR CYCLISTS

RESISTANCE TRAINING – THE NEXT LEVEL

The above reports are available at a cost of £29.99 each from Peak Performance (S/R), 33-41 Dallington Street, London, EC1V 0BB. Cheques should be made payable to Peak Performance.

CONTENTS

From the editor

These days you only need to have stepped your big toe over the threshold of the local gym to have heard all about the importance of core stability. In fact over the past 10 to 15 years this training concept has probably been more influential than any other training approach or marketing gimmick in breathing new life into the business of fitness and physical conditioning. It has fed the extraordinary growth in popularity of Pilates, and it has enabled us all to make connections between underlying fitness and high performance, injury avoidance, effective rehab and the reduction or cure of many every-day low-level pains and sources of physical discomfort.

So it feels as though a special report on the subject from the *Peak Performance* stable is well overdue. Well, here it is. We may have made you wait, but I think you'll find the results worthwhile. Our specialist sports therapists on *PP*'s sister publication *Sports Injury Bulletin* boast an impressive set of credentials and this collection represents the cream of their theoretical and working knowledge. I've deliberately included some of the slightly more technical physiotherapy material because I believe it offers really useful insights as to how sports therapists approach their work with clients. Everything in this report has highly practical relevance, right down to the invaluable set of training menus specially designed by our resident conditioning coach Raph Brandon, which take up the latter section of the report. This is as close as it gets to a body conditioning toolkit. I hope you get pleasure and good use from it.

Jane Taylor
Editor, Sports Injury Bulletin

We were not designed to sit around all day. So when we do, here's what happens

Sitting for long periods during the day can adversely affect your performance in your chosen sport and is quite often a predisposing factor in injury. Most of us are not professional athletes and spend large chunks of our day sitting hunched over a computer, in a vehicle or slumped on the sofa.

In most people, prolonged sitting will cause all or some of the following:

- tight hip flexor, hamstring and calf muscles
- tightness through the external hip rotator muscles, which can lead to restricted movement at the hip joint
- reduced extension through the lower back, causing stiffness
- stiffness in the mid (thoracic) spine
- tight and hunched shoulders with weak lower shoulder muscles
- tight and weak muscles at the back of the shoulder
- 'poked chin' posture and muscle imbalances in the neck and upper shoulders

The better the posture one can maintain during the day, the less likely it is that the above areas will become problematic. Conversely, the older the athlete and the more time spent sitting down over the years, the more ingrained these problems will be.

Let's consider Jack, a 30-year old delivery man who is trying to break a three-hour marathon time. His training is being increasingly affected by the low back and rear thigh discomfort he feels whenever he tries to run more than 15km. Jack sits most

Workplace rules for the sitting athlete

- Do not hold the phone receiver between shoulder and ear – use a headset
- Keep the computer mouse close enough that the elbow remains close in to the body
- Distribute all frequently used desk items evenly between left and right hand's reach
- Keep feet comfortably flat on the floor
- Ensure the chair has a relatively high and straight back-rest

of the day in quite poor posture, slouched over with his knees out to the side. All of which has produced some muscle imbalances, weaknesses and restrictions on his range of hip movement over the years.

Jack's daily training routine and flexibility programme need to be adjusted to combat the hours he spends sitting in the truck.

Now meet Denise, a 40-year-old lawyer and triathlete who spends hours on end, day and night, in front of a computer, and then more hours sitting on a bike – mostly in the hunched 'aero' position. Denise has an increased curvature of the mid-spine and a 'poked chin'. She also has several muscular imbalances and weaknesses, and flexibility limitations in her shoulders and mid-spine. These will undermine Denise's efficiency in her swimming stroke, and worse still make her a classic candidate for a shoulder impingement/tendinitis injury – the last thing she would want leading up to a qualifying race.

Just like Jack, Denise needs to undertake daily flexibility exercises and regular standing to combat the effects of spending so much time in a seated position. She'll also need an exercise programme to train postural and shoulder stability muscle groups.

Prolonged sitting has also been linked to acute muscle strains in dynamic sports, in particular hamstring strains. The lower back stiffness associated with sitting leads to altered nerve input into the rear thigh, the theory goes. This can manifest as increased muscle tone of the hamstrings, which will increase the risk of strain.

Sit up and pay attention

The solution starts with education. You must first learn how to put your body into good posture during the day; how to hold your spine in a correct position. Many people try to sit up tall by just leaning back from the base of the spine without altering their mid-spine or shoulder position. What you should be doing is finding a neutral lower back position and correcting your mid- to upper-back position, so you can effectively pull your shoulder blades down your back using the lower shoulder muscles, combatting the tendency to hunch forwards.

'Many people try to sit up tall by just leaning back from the base of the spine without altering their mid-spine or shoulder position'

However, it is very difficult to hold good posture if your workstation is poorly set up; for example with the keyboard too high or sat at an old chair with a sloping back-rest. A workplace assessment should help by modifying the height and placement of office equipment or introducing corrective devices to help with good sitting.

Jack may need a lumbar roll to get his low back out of flexion and a block next to the vehicle's door to prevent his knee and hip from falling outwards to the side all the time. Denise may need to raise the height of her monitor to eye level, lower the keyboard height so that her hands are at elbow level, and use a postural brace for her shoulder girdle and upper back while she is relearning to sit correctly. Seating wedges are very useful where chairs are too low (which forces you to sit with your knees higher than your hips and puts your lower back into flexion). The wedge is also very handy to correct bucket seats in cars.

Exercises to help you stay flexible

- Lie on your back over a rolled towel or high-density foam roller (placed perpendicular to spine) to stretch the mid-spine joints into extension
- Lie face down and push up into extension through the lower back
- Twist and stretch through the mid-spine
- Stand six inches away from a wall, knees slightly bent and back and shoulder blades flattened against the wall, then pull back the chin into the wall to reverse poor neck and upper-spine curvature
- Stretch your hip flexors, calves and hamstrings

Sean Fyfe

Pilates is the real deal in core conditioning. Find out why, and learn how to tell whether your instructor is up to scratch

In the world of working out, Pilates is high fashion. Once the best-kept secret of the dance community, Pilates has been discovered and embraced by singers, models, athletes and actors. But what exactly is Pilates – and does it really work?

At the outset it is important to understand that there are two distinct types of Pilates which you may come into contact with. The first kind is 'fitness' Pilates, offered through a variety of brands/training schools, and taught in classes at the gym, leisure centre or community hall, or available as a home video/DVD. The second type is 'clinical' Pilates, which has become increasingly integrated into mainstream sports therapy. This discipline is usually taught one-to-one, or under very close supervision within a small group, as part of a patient's rehabilitation from injury. It is the first category, fitness Pilates, that concerns us here.

Pilates in a nutshell

Fitness Pilates is a method of exercise and physical movement designed primarily to stabilise the trunk (the 'core'), producing more effective stretching, strengthening and balancing of the body. Through systematic practice of specific exercises coupled with focused breathing patterns, Pilates has proven itself invaluable as a fitness endeavour and an important adjunct to professional sports training.

It was developed in the 1920s by the German boxer, circus performer and exercise innovator Joseph Pilates, and began to gain a following when dancers he was working with discovered it could create long, lean muscles and a strong, streamlined physique. Pilates' system didn't really hit the big time, however, until the 1990s.

After years of high-impact, feel-the-burn fitness workouts, there was great appeal in a slower, safer approach to health and wellness. Fitness Pilates can condition the body from head to toe with a no- to low-impact approach suitable for all ages and abilities. It requires patience, attention to detail with your body and consistent practice, but results are guaranteed to follow if one sticks at it and does it right.

The kinds of results and benefits you can expect from an accurate, educated and well designed Pilates programme include:

- improving strength, flexibility and balance
- toning and building long, lean muscles without bulk
- challenging deep abdominal muscles to support the core
- engaging the mind and enhancing body awareness
- reducing stress, relieving tension, and boosting energy through deep stretching
- restoring postural alignment
- creating a stronger, more flexible spine
- promoting recovery from strain or injury
- increasing joint range of motion
- improving circulation
- enhancing mobility, agility and stamina
- improving the way your body looks and feels.

Behind each of these benefits there are physiological and technical justifications, but success depends entirely on understanding the basic principles and practices of Pilates, and doing it right.

Pilates is such a versatile exercise system that it is beneficial for a wide variety of conditions. Some fitness facilities target a particular kind of clientele or rehabilitative issue, such as pregnancy, back care, seniors, the unfit and so on. Pilates is also appealing because it can be practised in different contexts: at home in front of a video, as part of a class in a gym/health club, or in a studio setting. Exercises can be done on mats, with Swiss balls, elastic tubing or rings, or on some weird and wonderful contraptions unique to Pilates called Reformer, Trap Table, Wunda Chair and Thoracic Barrel.

Ideally fitness Pilates is practised in a studio under the careful supervision of a certified instructor. A well trained specialist knows how to tailor a Pilates regime to meet individual needs and abilities, monitoring movements to ensure correct technique for optimum results.

The emphasis of a good Pilates session is on quality (rather than quantity) of movement, not on how much you can sweat and lift but on how well you can stay true to the principles it espouses. Only certain types of yoga can deliver similar improvements.

Stability, flexibility, durability

The foundation stone of the Pilates movement is the concept of *core stability*. A stable trunk, or mid-section, is the best platform from which to develop whole-body muscular strength and endurance (durability), balance and flexibility. Having a stable 'centre' allows one to move in a way that reduces energy wastage (poor technique and fatigue), tissue overload (injury), and muscle confusion (poor alignment/ imbalance). Pilates' balanced approach ensures that no muscle group is overworked; the body operates as an efficient, holistic system in sport and daily activity.

In any context the body must have some degree of stability before it can function, whether it be gardening or sprinting (nowhere better on display than in slow-motion footage of the great US sprinter Michael Johnson, who had awesome trunk stability). The greater an athlete's initial levels of stability, the easier it is for their body to master the specific requirements of their sport. On the other hand, poor core stability will short-circuit any attempts to improve deficiencies in flexibility or durability.

Nowhere is this more true than with athletes hell-bent on pushing their bodies to the limit: without a stable trunk, you will endlessly battle with injury and poor performance, and will certainly never reach your full potential.

Hence, muscle and joint stability is the key prerequisite for the efficient development of muscle flexibility and durability. And the principles and equipment of fitness Pilates help to achieve this better than most, if not all, other exercise systems.

The Six Cs

There are several variations of Pilates principles, ranging from those that Joseph Pilates pioneered to contemporary adaptations incorporating modern understandings of fitness, anatomy and biomechanics. The six principles that I believe define Pilates best are:

Concentration – That all-important mind-body connection. Conscious focus on movement enhances body awareness. Focusing the brain on the body part enhances proprioception (sense of body position in space).

Control – It's not about intensity. Rather, it's about the empowerment of having a definite and positive impact on a body part by being able to isolate and work the body's critical stability muscles. Ideal technique brings safe, effective results.

Centring – A focus on the specific muscles that stabilise the pelvis and the shoulder blades underlies the development of a strong core and enables the rest of the body to function efficiently. The correct muscles must be taught to hold for extended periods of time at a low level. Consequently all action starts from a stable core.

Conscious breathing – Deep, conscious diaphragmatic patterns of inhaling initiate any movement, help activate deep stabilising muscles and keep you focused.

Core alignment – Maintaining a 'neutral' position (joints held in mid-position by deep stabilising muscles) is the key to proper alignment, and this leads to good posture. You'll be aware of the position of your head and neck on the spine and pelvis, right down through the legs and toes.

Co-ordination – Flowing movement results from brain and body working perfectly in synergy; the aim is smooth, continuous motion, rather than jarring repetitions. Pilates has a grace and elegance to its movement that comes from working 'smarter', not 'harder'. Repetition is used to 'cement' good movement into your brain.

These principles are quite different from other forms of exercise such as an aerobics class, running, or a weights session. However, Pilates can greatly enhance the benefits of other types of exercise. For example, when you have learnt how to use your abdominals properly to stabilise your trunk, even cardio-vascular exercise such as running becomes an avenue to further train your abs.

Having a stable 'centre' also allows one to more effectively stretch one's limbs. Many of the flexibility problems we see in the physiotherapy clinic have an instability component that must be resolved in order to stay more flexible and functional in the long term.

So there you have the basics. But they only tell us part of the story. If we are really going to understand the Pilates concept and what makes it work, we need to look at it with the critical eye of science.

Has fitness Pilates lost the plot?

Certainly some of what fitness Pilates purports to offer taps deeply into the fundamentals of how humans can improve, restore and maintain safe and efficient movement patterns. However, in its fervent attempt to grow rapidly as an industry, fitness Pilates is in danger of becoming its own worst enemy. By forgetting its basic practices and principles, it loses all of its power to transform, and thus creates disillusionment, and at worst, injury.

I speak from experience: working as a physiotherapist in the sports and fitness industry, I hear weekly about the injuries created in Pilates classes by well-meaning instructors with upwards of 30 people in their care. The most common complaint is low-back pain related to forward bending (flexion).

An example of this is an inflamed disc that creates pain and prevents full forward flexibility. Sitting becomes painful, and bending over or lifting can be even worse.

Yet I truly believe that, given some simple keys, many people can (and do) unlock the door to the many benefits listed above. The keys they need are *accuracy* and *specificity*.

Key 1: Accuracy

Accuracy relates to *how* fitness Pilates is taught: the method, the environment, the context. The success of the system relies heavily on the careful education and monitoring of a client by a correctly trained teacher. The question must be asked: does the advantage of teaching 30 clients in a class outweigh the disadvantages of 50 per cent to 90 per cent of those participants getting it wrong?

From experience, I know that it can take up to 30 minutes of one-to-one attention and direction from me before a patient learns to isolate and activate the correct muscles for even one new movement pattern.

And then they have to practise it! When working with a motivated client, I find that their body takes what it has learnt in our Pilates session and may do things differently for a day or two, until old, bad habits (eg, sitting stooped at a desk for eight hours, or standing 'lazily' with a child draped across a hip) undo the good we achieved.

I believe one-to-one training must remain the basic initial learning tool for the Pilates method.

Key 2: Specificity

Specificity relates to *what* is being taught. We're talking about the critical word in exercise philosophy here: *you get what you train*.

So, if you as a client are doing Pilates and strengthening the wrong abdominal muscle group, you will probably get good at tensing the wrong muscle, but never achieve correct stability. Or if you have not been shown correctly how to move around your pelvis in order to hold a neutral spine, your brain will learn an incorrect movement pattern and your body will be setting itself up for injury.

The greater the specificity, the greater chance of success with our goal to deliver true stability to our bodies.

Conclusion

The power of Pilates lies in the detail. The future credibility of the whole Pilates industry depends on not sacrificing specificity and accuracy, the two key elements that set it apart from other exercise fads and fashions, and make it such a potent tool for anyone interested in maintaining peak physical conditioning.

Ulrik Larsen

Fun and fashionable, are Swiss balls effective? The research findings may surprise you

In the past 10 years large inflatable plastic balls variously known as Swiss balls, fit balls or stability balls have become *de rigueur* gym equipment. Ranks of them line the back walls of class studios, a couple always lurk in the abs and stretch area and, increasingly, they are kept in the free weights room. They will also be found in any self-respecting sports physiotherapy clinic.

Over a very similar period of time, 'core stability' has invaded the world of recreational sport and fitness, transforming traditional approaches to training and keep fit at all levels of aspiration. And in the realm of core stability, Swiss balls have become indispensable, almost synonymous with the very concept. If you are serious about core conditioning, you work out using a Swiss ball.

But can these cheap, cheerful, oversized space hoppers justify their popularity in terms of effectiveness? Sports science research goes some way towards helping us resolve the issue of whether Swiss balls are beneficial or simply fashionable.

The fitness trainer Paul J Goodman[1] argues that Swiss ball-based exercises are the key to effective improvements in trunk strength. Because actions performed on the ball involve greater stimulation of the body's 'neuromuscular system', users develop better balance, co-ordination and proprioception (sense of bodily awareness in space), Goodman says. These assertions are not backed up by any research references – rather, they come from Goodman's experience of working with clients using Swiss balls.

Evidence to support the efficacy of Swiss ball exercises comes in a piece of research from a Canadian laboratory. Kathryn Clark and her research team at Dalhousie University's School of Health and Human Performance compared the electromyographic (EMG) activity of the upper abdominal (rectus abdominis) muscle during various abdominal exercises[2]. By measuring the level of electrical activity, EMG gives an indication of the degree of muscle activity going on. High levels of EMG are associated with high forces and a greater number of muscle fibres being recruited.

Clark's team analysed several abdominal exercises: the curl up (floor), Swiss ball curl up, reverse curl, ab roller curl up, Swiss ball roll-out to bridge, and supine leg-lower. The average level of EMG activity for three repetitions of each exercise was calculated as a percentage of each subject's maximum level of EMG activity.

The maximum EMG for the upper abdominal muscle was determined by the subject performing a 'maximal voluntary contraction' (strongest muscle force possible) during the ab crunch movement against an immovable resistance created by a trainer pushing down the subject's shoulders.

The researchers found that the Swiss ball curl up resulted in the highest EMG score out of all the ab exercises, at about 90 per cent of maximum EMG – significantly higher; for instance, than the ab curl on the floor, which recorded an EMG level of about 70 per cent.

Support for Clark's findings comes from another Canadian researcher, Stuart McGill [3]. His team also looked at the EMG activity of the Swiss ball ab curl versus the ab curl on the floor. McGill reports that the EMG activity of the upper abs and oblique muscles is greater when the ab curl is performed on the Swiss ball. Thumbs up for the Swiss ball so far.

Another piece of research looked at the Swiss ball from a different angle. David Behm and team, from the Memorial University of Newfoundland, compared how much muscle force was used to perform exercises under stable (on a bench) versus unstable (on a Swiss ball) conditions[4]. They examined muscle force and EMG of the front of thigh (quadriceps) muscle during leg extension and calf muscle during plantar-flexion (toe-pointing), in stable and unstable modes, also noting the electrical activity of the opposing (antagonist) muscles (hamstrings and dorsiflexors).

This produced some unexpected results. As might be expected, the leg extension and plantar-flexion forces were greater where the subject was stable, seated on the bench rather than on the Swiss ball. However, while the front-of-thigh and calf electrical activity was lower during the unstable movement, the EMG of the opposing muscles (hamstring and dorsiflexors) *increased*. This suggests that the level of activity of the main muscles (prime movers) is inhibited during unstable exercise, with increased muscular activity going on in the opposing muscles. So Swiss balls are not going to be the best way of developing prime-mover muscle strength.

‘The Swiss ball changes the task from pure leg extension to leg extension while controlling the body. In other words, stability/ proprioception rather than limb-strengthening’

The Newfoundland researchers did not measure the effect of the different training surfaces on core muscle EMG (such as the abdominals), but the likelihood is that it would have increased significantly on the Swiss ball, because the instability has the effect of spreading the forces over a greater number of joints and placing more stress on active stabilising muscles, thereby limiting the force directed through the prime-mover muscles.

In simple terms, the Swiss ball changes the task from pure leg extension to leg extension while controlling the body. It turns the movement into a stability/proprioception exercise rather than a limb-strengthening exercise.

So while this research does not support the use of Swiss ball for strength exercises of the leg muscles, it does indirectly support Swiss ball exercises for use in core stability programmes.

Together, these research findings will lend encouragement to devotees of Swiss ball training and the growing number of trainers and therapists who prescribe ball-based exercises most of the time for all muscle groups, in the belief that this will increase core stability and ‘make the exercise more functional’.

I routinely see athletes and gym users performing many

exercises on balls, including core strength, a range of dumb-bell upper body exercises such as bench press, and squatting movements. Before we leap in and endorse such an approach, a few questions and observations are in order.

Q: Does the Swiss ball automatically increase core muscle activation?

‘In most cases I have seen, the exerciser on the Swiss ball does not have sufficiently good technique to be gaining any significant benefit’

To answer this, look not at the theory, but at what happens in practice. Just because a research article suggests an increased core training effect can be gained does not mean that the average gym user or rehab patient will be able to reap those benefits. This is because it is the quality of the individual’s technique, not the equipment you use, that overwhelmingly determines how effective the exercise is.

Let’s take the Swiss ball ab curl, which the researchers have proved has a superior training effect to the version done lying on the floor. In most cases I have seen, the exerciser working out on the Swiss ball does not have sufficiently good technique to be gaining any significant benefit.

What normally occurs is that the exerciser simply pivots their low back around the curvature of the ball, levers their shoulders up and probably uses their hip flexors to help pull their trunk up. This lever action significantly reduces the load on the abdominals and side stomach (oblique) muscles.

These gym-goers have never been taught how to fix their pelvises using the buttock muscles (gluteals), so that the pelvis holds fast as the shoulders curl up off the ball. Unless you have this level of technique (which means, by the way, that you already have some core strength), you will be better off doing the exercise on the floor.

Swiss ball ‘roll ups’ – as I call the bad-technique version – are easy and anyone can do many repetitions without any benefit. Swiss ball curl ups – fixing the pelvis with strict technique – are tough, and sets of 10 reps will be challenging for most people.

Using the Swiss ball, then, is no guarantee of increased training success. Balls change exercises – usually making them more advanced – and you will need superior strength and technique to perform the modified exercises effectively. Instructors should always put technique and correct muscle recruitment ahead of any 'favoured' piece of equipment. If the exerciser cannot use the targeted muscle groups effectively or control the unstable surface adequately, then the exercise will not have the desired effect and the instructor should find an alternative.

Q: Are Swiss ball exercises suitable for people with low back problems?

If Swiss ball curl ups (with good technique) are very effective at challenging the abdominals, McGill's research alerts us to increased levels of trunk muscle 'co-contraction', which is associated with increased spinal loading. This is important for anyone undertaking injury rehab for their back: you will need to take great care not to overstress your healing back when you use a Swiss ball.

McGill also challenges another contemporary instability fashion, for prescribing Swiss balls or air cushions as suitable sitting surfaces in the office (a Swiss ball plus frame is supposed to replace your office chair). The rationale is to help the individual strengthen their trunk muscles during daily activity and keep their spine mobile throughout the day. McGil's research shows that spinal loads are greater on unstable surfaces compared to sitting on a chair. He would not recommend this for his patients.

Q: Why perform leg and arm exercises on the Swiss ball?

It is very common these days to see people in the gym doing traditional strength exercises on Swiss balls, often using dumb-bells or similar free weights, in the belief that this will make the actions somehow more 'functional' or help them further improve their core stability.

Yet as we have seen above, the Newfoundland study found that the specific strength-training effect using Swiss balls is reduced, as exercise stresses are dissipated throughout the body.

The amount of weight lifted in a shoulder press exercise on a Swiss ball is significantly less than when sitting on a bench.

There is little added benefit, in fact. The dumb-bell bench press, for instance, already requires co-ordination of shoulder and elbow and stability from the trunk, even when performed on the stable bench. When the exercise is transferred to a lying position on the ball, the reality is that the leg muscles are quite active and provide much of the stabilising function to control the moving ball under the spine as the dumb-bells are pressed up and down. This is because the legs are the natural anchors when lying on your back on a ball.

Overall, then, I would argue that it is more efficient to lift heavier weights and gain the full strength benefit with traditional (and stable) leg and arm exercises, and then complement these with specific exercises for the trunk muscles which are guaranteed to target the core. More research is needed to establish the full range of benefits and limitations of using Swiss balls, but in the absence of scientific support, you would do well not to assume that everything done on a ball adds value to your training regime. Some of it may do (if you are already advanced enough in your fitness and technique to cope with it); other exercises will do you little or no good and if you have a low back injury you may be impeding the healing process.

Raphael Brandon

References

1. Goodman P, *Performance Training Journal of the US National Strength and Conditioning Association*, vol2 no6 p9-25
2. Clark *et al*, *Journal of Strength and Conditioning Research* 2003 17(3), 475-483
3. McGill S, 'Low Back Disorders', *Human Kinetics* 2002
4. Behm D *et al*, *Journal of Strength and Conditioning Research* 2002 16(3), 416-422

The Swiss Ball Curl Up – here's how to do it properly

Muscles involved: Upper abdominals (rectus abdominis)
Side abdominals (obliques)

The curl up involves forward bending (flexion) of the mid (thoracic) spine, lifting the weight of the shoulders and head using the upper abs assisted by the side abs. The advantage of the ball is that the mid-spine can work through a greater range of movement, starting from slightly extended through to fully flexed. This only works, however, if you can 'fix' your lumbar spine by keeping your pelvis still relative to the ball. Correct technique should also ensure that your shoulders and neck do not assist your abs in doing the work.

Purpose: A good way to progress the loading and demands of the standard ab curl exercise. Useful for sport-specific training for advanced core strength or at the end of a rehabilitation programme for a core stability progression.

Suitability: Strong exercisers with no low back symptoms.

Start position

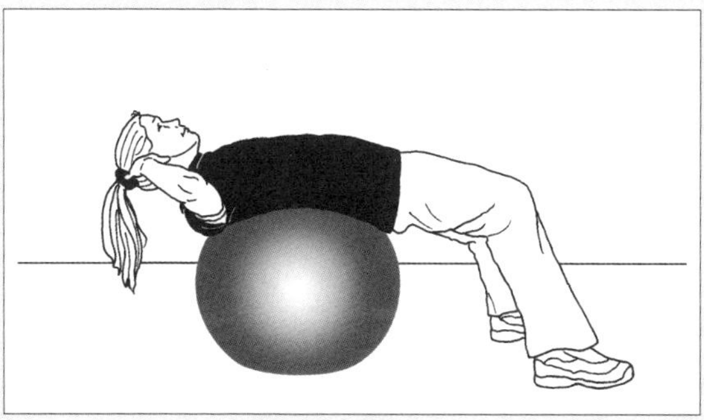

- Lie on your back on the ball. Knees bent and feet comfortably flat on the floor, shoulder-width apart for stability.
- Adjust your pelvis so your low back (lumbar spine) is in the neutral position, squeeze your buttock muscles and engage your deep abdominals (transversus and pelvic floor) to lock this position tightly.
- Lift your head slightly and bring your chin towards your chest. Fix your neck position as though you're holding an apple between your chin and neck.
- Place your hands to your ears and open your arms so your elbows point to the sides. Fix this arm position as well.

Curl up movement

- *Slowly*, focusing on your abdominals, curl your upper back off the ball. Do not move any other body part, keeping your arms, shoulders and neck and legs relaxed as the abs pull you up.
- If done correctly, your head and arms will curl up as one unit with your shoulders.
- Maintain the buttock and pelvic floor squeeze to keep your pelvis in neutral and to prevent it moving down the ball.
- Pause for a count of one at the top.

Return movement

- Slowly, again focusing on the abdominals, lower your upper back down until it is slightly extended (slightly arching back).
- Do not move your head or arms. You should return to exactly the same position as you started from.
- Keep the low back fixed in position.

Sets and reps

By eliminating movement around the ball (whereby you can lever yourself up), and by keeping your head still, the exercise is significantly more difficult than most people experience while performing it wrongly. Start with sets of 10 repetitions and progress to 20 reps. Once you can achieve three sets of 20, you may need to add weight to progress. You can hold a dumb-bell behind your head (again ensuring you do not lift with your arms) to add load to the curl up.

Simple twisting movements, performed correctly, can develop significant core strength. Here's why

Core stability training has come in a number of guises over the years, according to whatever modality happens to be the fashion of the moment. Most Swiss ball programmes, Pilates and other core workouts deliver useful benefits in both physical preparation and injury management. They offer a lot of variety – and there are some things you can do on a Swiss ball or Pilates Reformer that you simply cannot do on any other apparatus.

As the stream of new fads in equipment and training styles shows no sign of slowing, it is useful to return to basics and gain a little education about how the low back (lumbo-sacral spine) and its supporting muscle system work. This article introduces some important research done in recent years which helps us gain a much clearer practical understanding of how the low back and pelvis work, and therefore what kinds of training are most likely to have a positive impact on core strength and stability. This research introduces the anatomical concept of 'myofascial slings'.

Myofascial slings

The concept of myofascial slings comes out of the work done by Andre Vleeming and others on sacro-iliac joint (SIJ) stability. Contrary to what old rheumatologists will tell you, the sacro-iliac joints – which connect the fused section of the lower spine (the sacrum) to the pelvic/hip bones on either side – do need to move during normal daily activities such as walking and running.

It is both necessary and desirable that the sacro-iliac joints move, because they need to act as shock absorbers between the lower limbs and spine, and also as a way of providing proprioceptive (body positioning awareness) feedback for co-ordinated movement and control between the trunk and lower limbs.

'It is both necessary and desirable that the sacro-iliac joints move, because they need to act as shock absorbers between the lower limbs and spine'

As the SIJ is capable of movement, that movement needs to be properly controlled, as with any of the body's joints. Some control comes through the natural architecture of the low back and pelvis, but more is possible by using the surrounding muscle, ligament and connective tissue system (myofascial slings) to provide compression on the joints. This is important because we can influence the effectiveness of the compression through exercise and retraining after injury. The three muscle systems or 'slings' that help to stabilise the pelvic girdle are known as:

- the posterior oblique sling;
- the anterior oblique sling; and
- the posterior longitudinal sling.

Key training principles

1. Stay upright

Keep the compression load vertical: as most athletic endeavours and functional daily activities are done upright, most of the 'core' training work should also be done upright. It is also important to stand, rather than sit, so that you are able to transmit load through the legs. Ground reaction force when standing is transferred up the upper leg bone (femur), into the hip and the pelvic bones. This is met by the downward force of gravity acting on the trunk. This allows the SIJ to be held stable by using its natural architecture when standing, as the sacrum sits nicely into the corresponding surface of the pelvis/hip in this position.

Furthermore, the shock-absorbing intervertebral discs of the lower (lumbar) spine prefer the compression force that standing provides, rather than shear (sliding) force or tensile (pulling) force. Most damaging shear force occurs when the vertebrae slide against each other and shear the adjoining intervertebral disc – as happens when the body is horizontal (the position used for many Swiss ball exercises). Tensile force occurs when the lumbar spine is bent forwards or backwards (flexed or extended).

2. Work in neutral

Keep the spine in neutral. The most common way to damage intervertebral discs is to have the spine flexed, as you do when bent over. In this position the pressure inside the disc increases significantly; with added compression this position can cause discs to bulge. So it is important to keep the spine away from full flexion and extension positions, to avoid repeated microtrauma to discs, vertebrae and ligaments.

3. Learn to contract stomach muscles

Maintain the upper abdominals (rectus abdominis) in static contraction. Many elite athletic endeavours require that the abdominals work statically (isometrically). This allows the stomach muscle to provide a stable anchor for the powerful side trunk (oblique) muscles to generate force. The rectus anchors the obliques via lateral tendons and this design allows force to be transferred across to the oblique muscles.

Training the myofascial slings

With close attention to good technique, the simple twisting exercise in the diagram *(see overleaf)* is a good way of training the myofascial slings. The key principles apply as follows:

1. The exercise is performed standing up.
2. Bend slightly at knee and hip. This will pre-tense the buttocks (gluteus maximus) and front of thigh muscles (quadriceps), which in turn will help to create a chain of stability and tension through the posterior oblique sling.

3. Adopt a slightly forward leaning position with a gentle forward pelvic tilt. This activates the deep short muscles of the lower back (part of the posterior longitudinal sling).
4. There is trunk rotation against resistance. This activates the side stomach muscles (part of the anterior oblique sling). The upper stomach muscle must be statically contracted to provide a stable base for the obliques to work from. It is also important to activate the lower stomach muscle (the transversus abdominis) in a 'hollowing' action.
5. The broomstick sits on the shoulders, and is pulled into the shoulders to help secure the stability of the posterior oblique sling.

How to perform the exercise

This exercise was originally developed at the Australian Institute of Sport in Canberra. The diagram and points 1 to 5 above will guide you on correct form. Tape or otherwise fix the resistance bands firmly to the broomstick. An appropriate level of resistance (band strength and length) should allow you to perform 3 sets x 10 reps without great difficulty. Progress from there. Watch out for the following points to maintain good technique:

- Keep the front of thigh and buttock muscles tight
- Keep lower stomach (transversus) hollow and tense the upper stomach (rectus abdominis)
- Don't rotate the pelvis, just the trunk. If you have trouble achieving this, perch your buttocks on the back of a chair, which will help you to keep your hips stable while you get used to twisting through the trunk alone
- Maintain a slight arch in the lower back (neutral position)
- Keep looking straight ahead, do not allow your head to turn as your trunk rotates
- Keep the broomstick firm on your shoulders.

Programming

Note: one full repetition of this exercise involves rotating from X degrees backward trunk rotation to X degrees forward trunk rotation, and then returning to the backward start point.

Beginners

- Use a single band.
- Move through a small range of rotation 10 degrees to 10 degrees each direction (total arc of 20 degrees).
- Perform 3 sets of 10 reps each direction (band at left, then band at right).

Intermediate

- Use two bands, one either side of the broomstick.
- Rotate through 20 degrees to 20 degrees
- Perform 3 sets of 10 reps in each direction

Advanced

- Can double up number of bands (or more, and/or use tougher bands etc), depending on your rotation strength
- extend range of rotation up to 45 degrees to 45 degrees.
- Perform 3 sets of 10 reps in each direction.

Modifications

1. Place one foot on a step to increase the range of hip flexion. This is particularly effective for sports requiring stability in positions of hip flexion, eg: rowing and cycling.
2. Decrease the width of the base of support by adopting a lunge stride position

Chris Mallac

Myofascial slings: further reading

- Lavignolle, Vital J M, Senegas J *et al* (1983) 'An approach to the functional anatomy of the sacro-iliac joints in vivo'. *Anatomica Clinica* 5: 169-176.
- Richardson C A, Jull G A (1995) 'Muscle control-pain control. What exercise should you prescribe?' *Manual Therapy* 1: 2-10.
- Pool-Goudzwaard A L, Vleeming A, Stoeckart R, Snijders C J and Mens J M A (1998) 'Insufficient lumbopelvic stability: a clinical, anatomical and biomechanical approach to 'a-specific' low back pain'. *Manual Therapy* 3(1): 12-20.
- Vleeming A, Stoeckart R, Volkers A C W, Snijders C A (1990a) 'Relation between form and function in the sacro-iliac joint. Part 1: Clinical anatomical concepts'. *Spine* 15(2): 130-132.
- Vleeming A, Volkers A C W, Snijders C A Stoeckart R (1990b) 'Relation between form and function in the sacro-iliac joint. Part 2: Biomechanical concepts'. *Spine* 15(2): 133-136.

Weak buttocks ruin the runner. Discover how, by firming up your butt, you can boost your performance

How many regular runners would suspect that the upper buttock muscle (gluteus medius) is the culprit in very many running overuse injuries? This fact is less surprising once you understand that during running you are always either completely in the air or dynamically balanced on one leg – and in both circumstances gluteus medius is a key muscle.

Situated on the upper edge of the hip *(see below)*, gluteus medius is responsible for lifting the leg away from the body (abduction), helping it to rotate inwards and outwards, and, crucially, keeping the pelvis stable in certain situations, including the stance phase of running.

During right stance phase, for instance, the muscle contracts to slow the downward motion of the left side of the pelvis so that the pelvis doesn't tilt heavily towards the ground. If the gluteus medius is not functioning well enough to achieve this control, the athlete is said to have a 'Trendelenburg gait'. Often, but not always, the same weakness may be noticeable in

Gluteus medius: fibres

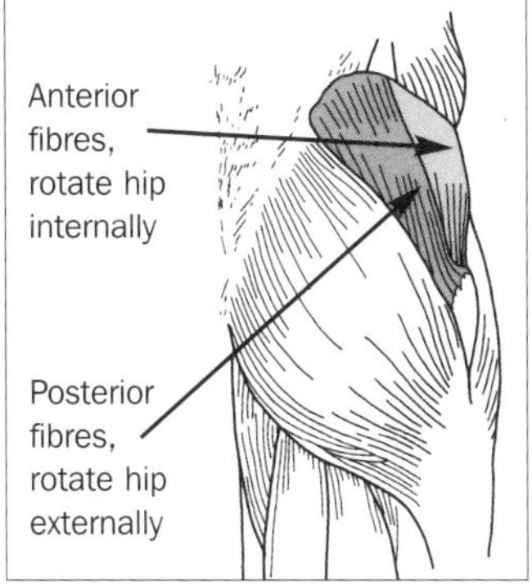

Table 1: Adaptations to weak gluteus medius in stance phase	
Adaptations	**Areas at risk of structural overload**
1. Trendelenburg (heavy tilting of pelvis)	Lumbar spine, sacro-iliac joint (SIJ), greater trochanter bursa, insertion of muscle on greater trochanter, overactivity of piriformis and tensor fascia lata (TFL)
2. Medial (inwards) knee drift	Compression of lateral tibiofemoral compartment (outer side of knee), knee joint, patellar tendon and fat pad, pes anserinus, iliotibial band (ITB)
3. Lateral (outward) knee drift	Compression of medial tibiofemoral compartment (inner edge of knee), ITB, posterolateral compartment (outer rear corner), popliteus
4. Same-sided shift of trunk	Lumbar spine (increased disc and facet joint compression), SIJ (increased shear)

walking, producing a waddling motion or, in extreme cases, a limp.

Runners who have a weak or easily fatigued gluteus medius are likely to make various adaptations to their technique, which can hide the true reason for a running injury. Table 1 lists the adaptations or cheating movements that occur through the stance phase of running.

Adaptations 2 and 3 clearly cannot occur simultaneously, but a runner's technique may demonstrate a combination of adaptations, such as a mild Trendelenburg, inwards knee drift and a same-sided trunk shift.

In my experience, runners with poor dynamic pelvic stability, for which gluteus medius is vital, will decrease their stride length and adopt a more shuffling pattern to reduce the ground reaction force at contact and thereby the muscle control required to maintain pelvic posture.

Weakness in gluteus medius will have implications all the way down the kinetic chain. With Adaptation 2, for instance, the buttock weakness will produce inward drifting and rotating throughout the leg during running, which will leave the runner at increased risk of any condition relating to excessive and/or prolonged pronation of the foot, such as shin splints (medial tibial stress syndrome) or Achilles tendinitis.

A highly informative study by Fredericson *et al* (2000)[1] upholds the idea that gluteus medius weakness is a contributing factor in ITB friction syndrome; confirms that injured and uninjured sides can be compared to determine weakness; and endorses retraining for strength gains as an effective treatment.

Fredericson measured hip abductor strength in a group of injured male and female subjects, and found an average deficit of 2 per cent in gluteus medius strength on the injured side compared to the uninjured. After a six-week retraining programme, average hip abductor torque improved by 34.9 per cent for females and 51.4 per cent for males; 22 of the 24 injured athletes were able to return to running pain free. Most importantly, at a six-month follow-up no injury recurrences were reported.

Case study: Chris's knee pain

Chris presented to the sports injury clinic after experiencing pain on the inner side of his right knee resulting from the first four weeks of training for his lifetime goal: a marathon. His activity history was of upper-body weight training, not running. An assessment revealed tenderness on the joint line; pain and an inability to achieve a full squat or knee flexion; and discomfort when tested for damage to the meniscus (shock-absorbing cartilage).

Chris also demonstrated an inability to activate gluteus medius when he was lying on his side and lifting his upper leg; and a complete lack of control with single leg squat and single leg knee bends: he was unable to maintain pelvic alignment or keep his knee tracking in line with his foot. Because of poor movement control at his hip, his knee was falling inwards and his already flat foot was pronating further.

A video assessment revealed a classic case of Adaptation 3: extremely forward tilted trunk position; and the right knee being thrown outwards on ground contact.

It was now clear why his right knee was so irritated. Every stance phase, the meniscus and articular cartilage were being compressed. Trying to train for a marathon with this level of control and technique would have severe consequences for the long-term health of Chris's knee.

We had to advise Chris to abort his marathon campaign for the moment. Still determined to achieve his dream, he began a retraining programme. The initial aim of the regime was to gain activation and strength in gluteus medius while being able to maintain correct alignment. To start with, Chris did the clam exercise *(see opposite)*, feeling his own gluteus medius to check it was activating properly; and practised holding a single-leg semi squat position on a 15-degrees decline board, using a mirror for visual feedback on his lower limb posture. The decline board helps to increase activation of vastus medialis (the lower quad muscle) and it also offset Chris's limited ankle flexibility, which would otherwise compromise his ability to perform the squat with correct technique.

Chris gradually lengthened the time he could maintain the static squat and deepened the squat position. He also increased repetitions of both exercises. The clam exercise was progressed to side-lying abduction *(see opposite)* to increase the load, and Chris began dynamic single-leg squats, slowly but steadily improving his level of control and squat depth. We then introduced single-leg knee bends on the decline board. These differ from the single-leg squat in that the body is held upright and the knee should bend forward *past* the toes – but still tracking in alignment. The movement pattern is slightly different from the squat, with a close focus on control of the knee.

Once the gluteus-medius and single-leg control reached a suitable level, we introduced more dynamic exercises to retrain the muscle's timing and effectiveness as a shock absorber on impact. This must be done with a mirror. The first exercise is single-leg jump and hold (ie, hop and hold), ensuring correct alignment is maintained. The athlete should focus on pre-tensing gluteus medius and VMO (lower quad) before impact.

Once this was achieved, we progressed to continual single-leg jumping (hopping), before allowing Chris to return to running. During running, the athlete should concentrate on pre-tensing before heel strike and maintaining alignment.

Chris's training programme now includes the single-leg squats and knee bends to maintain and improve the strength and endurance of his gluteus medius in conjunction with the other crucial muscles that are required for lower limb/pelvic posture during running. His training mileage is increasing steadily as he builds up to his big day.

This rehabilitation programme was a joint effort over three months between physiotherapist and podiatrist. Once a reasonable amount of control was reached, an orthotic (shoe insert) was introduced to help Chris maintain alignment, which in theory should also help the activation of his key stability muscles.

Two exercises to build gluteus medius strength

The Clam

Lie on the uninjured side, with hips bent to about 30 degrees, knees bent, and hips, knees and feet all stacked in line. Open the knees while keeping the heels firmly together and, most importantly, keeping the pelvis completely still. Hold, then close the knee again, under control. Repeat, eg, 10 times.

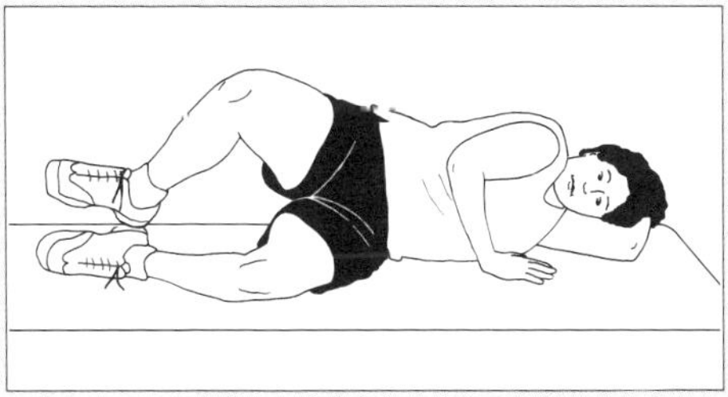

Side-lying leg raise

Lie on uninjured side, with lower leg bent at the knee. Top leg should be straight and lined up slightly behind the line of the back. Lift the top leg, without allowing the top hip to hitch, or tilt forwards or backwards. Hold the lifted leg, then return slowly under control. Good gluteus medius strength should enable you to hold this lifted leg position for 30 seconds, maintaining good pelvic alignment throughout.

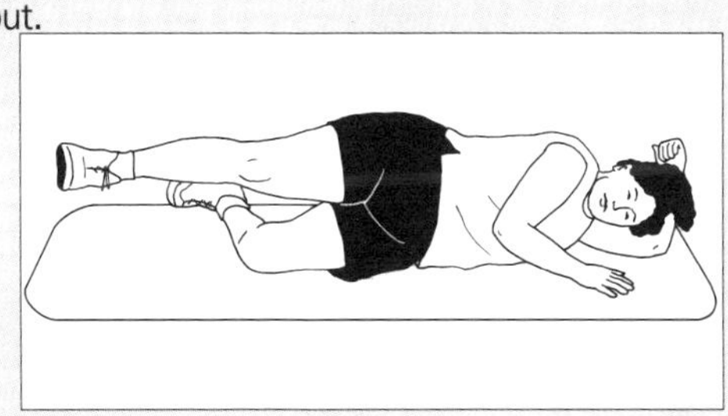

Sean Fyfe

Reference

1. Fredericson M, Cookingham CL, Chaudhari AM, Dowdell BC, Oestreicher N, Sahrmann SA, 'Hip abductor weakness in distance runners with iliotibial band syndrome'. *Clin J Sport Med*. 2000 Jul;10(3):169-75.

The tale of Anna's dodgy shoulders holds two lessons: the importance of good stability and the importance of a rigorous approach by your sports therapists

Anna, a tall, slim 15 year old, arrived for her appointment to see me with her mother. Together they explained that she had a national swim meet in a fortnight, but that her shoulders were really giving her problems – and had been doing so for about three months. During that time Anna had increased her training ahead of the state championships, where she had performed surprisingly well in various freestyle and medley events, considering how little training she had done previously.

Anna seemed quite gangly, with stooping posture, a gait that looked very sloppy (knees bending backwards and unstable pelvis) with quite big feet… it was as though she was designed for the pool!

She complained that her shoulders clicked, and occasionally felt like they 'popped out of joint' when she was doing a hard sprint session. They tended to hurt mainly as an ache, often after she had cooled off, but occasionally during her warm-up. They could feel very tight when she woke up.

A GP they had visited prescribed anti-inflammatory medication, told her she had rotator cuff tendinitis (inflammation), and sent her for stretching and ultrasound treatment. Anna's coach was keen to talk with me about what was going on with his star swimmer and whether she would be ready for the nationals in two weeks' time.

Deciding what's wrong

As soon as a clinician has been presented with the story of the injury, their brain begins to play with various diagnostic scenarios. This process, called 'clinical reasoning', weighs up the subjective (from interview) and objective (from hands-on testing or other investigative procedures) information from the client, and gradually develops an evidence-based rationale for the most likely diagnosis. The diagnosis forms the building block for all future management; hence: *no accurate diagnosis, no good result*.

In this instance, based on what we knew from Anna's story, we needed to assess the validity of the following possible diagnoses, in order of greatest likelihood (there are other possible shoulder pathologies, but I believed these were the most likely):

Multi-directional instability (MDI) of the gleno-humeral joint

This was the strongest likelihood. The fact that Anna was having trouble in both shoulders implied a likely genetic/familial component and MDI tends to occur on both sides in shoulders where there is a genetic tendency towards hyper-mobility. Excessive translation (shearing movement) and poor centring of the head of humerus (the 'ball' in the shoulder socket) in all directions leads to gradual destruction of the cartilaginous rim (the labrum) and rotator cuff tendon. Pain and clicking result, with the head of humerus in effect repeatedly popping slightly in and out of the joint during the swimming stroke.

Uni-directional instability of gleno-humeral joint

Excessively protracted posture (rounded shoulders destroy the swimmer!) can cause the centre of rotation of the head of humerus gradually to drift forwards. The subscapularis muscle loses its ability to control it, straining on the joint capsule and loosening, which soon leads to instability. Eventually the head of humerus would start to pop out, or the rotator cuff tendon would impinge (catch) under the acromion (top outer edge of the shoulder blade), resulting in pain and clicking. Uni-directional instability would be more likely to occur in one overloaded shoulder, especially on the non-dominant arm in a bilateral sport, not in two.

Superior labrum anterior posterior (SLAP) lesion
Looseness at the front of the shoulder joint can also overload the long head of biceps tendon and the lower part of the joint capsule, which ends up destabilising the connection of the cartilage on the rim to the bony glenoid. However, this type of shoulder injury more commonly afflicts throwing athletes and, again, usually presents on just one side.

Rotator cuff impingement or tendinitis
Based on Anna's account of her symptoms, this is likely to be a secondary problem caused by instability: uni- or multi-directional. In fact gleno-humeral instability is a much under-diagnosed cause of rotator cuff impingement or tendinitis. Anna, at the age of 15, is very unlikely to have tearing or significant degenerative change of her rotator cuff, although it may be inflamed.

Clinical testing

Tests done by an experienced physiotherapist will greatly help to decide or confirm their hypothesis. We used the following tests to help us work out which of the above diagnoses best described Anna's problem.

Sulcus test (gently drawing the head of humerus out of the socket) determines the extent of MDI and loss of normal negative-suction joint pressure, and compares joint looseness on left and right sides of the body. We did other general hypermobility testing (eg, elbows and thumbs) to confirm Anna's hypermobile status (which is shared by 10 per cent to 20 per cent of the population).

Anterior laxity testing: (moving the extended arm through various positions) This test will determine how far the head of humerus passively moves forwards in its socket; the results are graded l to lll, depending on the distance it moves relative to the width of the head of humerus. The physio would also do forwards and backwards moves of the head of humerus in sitting, to help work out the direction and extent of laxity.

Apprehension testing: the test is positive if a backwards (posterior) glide of the head of humerus in a 'stop' sign takes away discomfort.

Posterior laxity testing: determines the extent of instability in the context of MDI.

Long head of biceps: (moving the bent arm against resistance in various positions). Clicking and pain might reveal the compromised integrity of the bicep muscle attachment at the shoulder rim.

Cervical and thoracic spine: The therapist can feel for stiffness through the mid- to upper spine. Stiffness here is very common and disrupts the normal movement of the shoulder joint.

We also did tests for:

- rotator cuff flexibility
- impingement
- stability

Short-term (pre-competition) aims of management

Having done the above tests we concluded that Anna's primary problem was indeed a multi-directional instability of the shoulder joint, rooted in being genetically hypermobile. This had led to secondary irritation and impingement of the rotator cuff tendon.

Once we were fairly certain of our diagnosis, we devised a management plan, initially focused on the big upcoming competition; thereafter looking to provide a long-term resolution of Anna's injuries. Trying to be realistic about what we could achieve in two weeks, we limited our pre-competition strategy to three areas:

1. Establish accurate diagnosis as early as possible

This was essential. It might require a second opinion from a sports physician, and possibly scans: ultrasound for rotator cuff tendon integrity, CT arthrogram/ MRI for labral (cartilage) tears, X-ray to view shallowness of the glenoid socket

2. Minimise short-term pain and further joint breakdown

We used trigger-point work and massage on the rotator cuff to eliminate pain from active movements, impingement positions and finally, Anna's swimming stroke. We undertook deep-tissue massage of the key back, chest, neck, shoulder and arm muscles. We mobilised the mid- and upper spine.

We immediately stopped Anna from continuing any harmful or aggravating practices, such as bad sleeping positions (with her shoulders in extreme positions and being leant on badly); carrying too heavy a school back pack; and any risks from other sports she might be playing.

We assessed Anna's stretching regime, believing it was likely that most of her stretches would be damaging her because of her poor control. As a better alternative we taught her to do self-trigger point therapy and massage.

We taped the shoulder blades for support out of the pool and to help Anna re-educate her posture. In the pool we experimented with a different kind of tape for joint support and to help her get feedback on joint position.

We discussed with Anna's coach a short-term reduction in her training load and intensity for pain management, and established a focus on quality not quantity during the run-up to the competition (for instance, minimising her butterfly training because of the greater loads this stroke places on the joint structures at the front of the shoulder).

We used non-steroidal anti-inflammatories and ice after training as required.

'Anna, at the age of 15, is very unlikely to have tearing or significant degenerative change to her rotator cuff, although it may be inflamed'

3. Educate Anna, her parents and her coach

The key points to convey were:

- the nature of the shoulder problem, especially how normal and unstable shoulders differ structurally;
- the importance of posture;
- an overall appreciation of the strengths and weaknesses of her body-type: her flexibility, which is such a natural plus in her swimming, needed to be balanced by stability and strength. Muscle control and strength must become her focus or she would never establish herself as a competitive swimmer. She needed a paradigm shift from concentrating mainly on flexibility to focusing instead on technique, co-ordination, warm-up drills and home-based self-massage and triggering to deal with tightness.

Her long-term goal had to be prevention and management. She would have to learn to stay on top of it by doing positive things for her shoulders, especially when they were feeling good.

Long-term (post-competition) aims of management

We are confident that a full resolution of Anna's shoulder problem is possible, with a return to symptom-free swimming, and a full training and competitive load. She will probably need, however, to maintain a preventive regime to ensure she stays injury-free. As with many athletes who have had sports injuries, Anna will have to get used to taking responsibility for preventing a recurrence until the day she decides to hang up her goggles for good.

We had three main long-term strategic goals.

1. maximise the muscular control of her shoulder joint

This involves developing, with Anna, her parents and her coach, a graduated plan to combat weaknesses and active instability.

The retraining work should start with local stability muscles, working around three key areas:

- trunk (transversus abdominis)
- scapula (lower trapezius and serratus anterior)
- head of humerus (subscapularis)

The business of getting an athlete to learn how to activate correctly these tonic (holding) stability muscles is a fairly precise clinical science that may require the use of equipment and manual feedback by a skilled physiotherapist.

This stability and strengthening work would take three to six months, divided into three phases:

Activation of correct muscles, as described above. For instance, if Anna didn't learn to activate the muscles controlling her shoulder blades, she would perpetually tend towards downward rotation, making it impossible for her subscapularis muscle to control the head of humerus properly. So the mid-lower traps (upward rotators of the shoulder blade) must be trained over the rhomboids for stability *(see exercise 1, page 57)*.

Recruitment of same stability muscles within rehab and dry-land swimming drills. As local stability improves, the exercises should gradually stress global strength and stability muscles. The quality of control remains a high priority as the exercises are progressed *(see exercises 2a to 2c)*.

Training – stability and strength gains on land would be incorporated into gradually increasing intensity and distance in the pool. As long as Anna's shoulders are asymptomatic after a few months of rehab training, her swimming training and competition schedule should not need to be affected. Pool drills will further develop her awareness and endurance. During warm-up, Anna should do low-load stability drills rather than stretching, to activate the brain-body connection.

Regardless of whether the shoulders are symptomatic, Anna's off-season period will need to include a few weeks of stability and strength work in the lead-up to the beginning of swim training.

'We assessed Anna's stretching regime, believing it was likely that most of her stretches would be damaging her because of her poor control'

2. Resolve technique issues

Video analysis would be introduced through all three phases of rehabilitation training, in close liaison with the coach. It is critical that an athlete's learning and awareness of good stability runs alongside their correction of poor technique, so they can understand and apply the muscle retraining to make necessary but often subtle changes to movement mechanics. For instance, learning to hold the trunk and shoulders still while 'catching' the water and pulling through directly enhances scapular stability.

3. Long-term flexibility management

Anna's priorities would be her thoracic spine, back, chest and neck musculature, to enhance the stability of her trunk, shoulder blade and head of humerus. She would be likely to need maintenance physio and massage, especially in periods of intense training and competition, in order to remain symptom-free.

If Anna can overcome the obstacles at this stage of her career, she could open up for herself the opportunity to achieve what the shoulders of Ian Thorpe have: genetic hyperflexibility coupled with fantastic control and strength, leading to top-level success.

Ulrik Larsen

Exercise 1: scapular stability

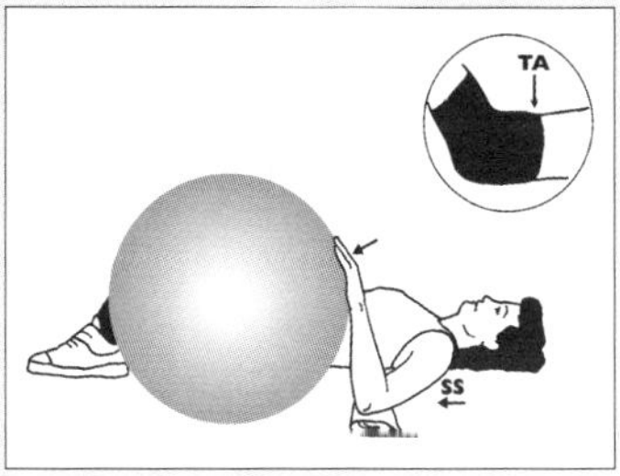

Lie with knees bent, feet on floor, pelvis in neutral. One arm rests at 60 degrees out to the side, with elbow on a rolled towel to set the shoulder blade in neutral. Hand rests on Swiss ball at side of body. Gently press hand into ball to activate the subscapularis muscle as the shoulder ball and socket are held in neutral. Transversus (TA) is actively stabilising. Mid and lower traps (SS) are actively maintaining scapular stability. Perform 10 x 10sec static presses.

Exercises 2a to 2c: rehab with stability

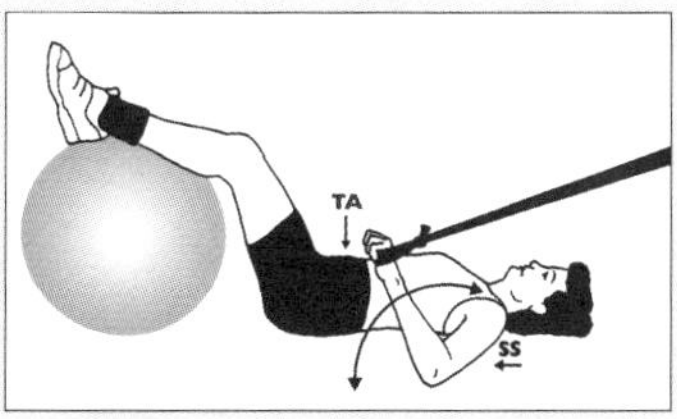

2a: Lie with calves resting on Swiss ball, pelvis in neutral, arm out to the side as with Exercise 1. Lower arm rotates through elbow pivot, pulling against a resistance band, from upright down towards the floor, maintaining full scapular and transversus control. Return to upright to repeat the movement. Sets, reps, intensity of resistance can all be altered for progression.

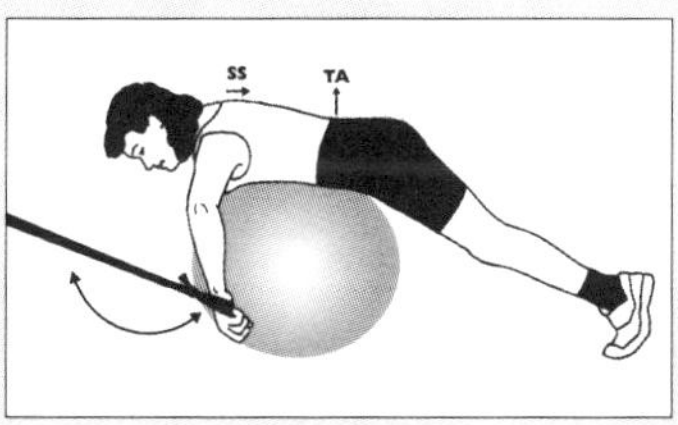

2b: Lie prone with ball under chest, legs hip-width apart, pelvis in neutral. Arm rotates against resistance band through elbow pivot as shown, maintaining full transversus and scapular control. Sets, reps, intensity of resistance can all be altered for progression.

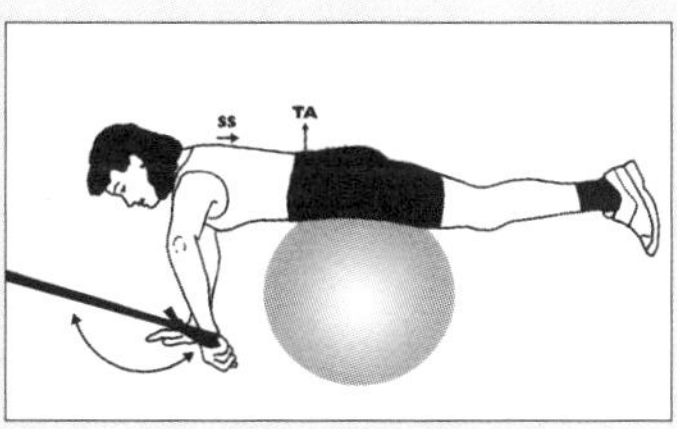

2c: Lie prone with ball under pelvis, body balanced, with non-active arm providing fixed point of stability. Execute 'stroke' against resistance band as shown, maintaining full transversus and scapular control. Sets, reps, intensity of resistance can all be altered for progression. You can also add in leg movement (freestyle kick action) to make it harder.

This off-the-shelf system can revolutionise your approach to stability workouts and deliver invaluable results

If you have ever had a sports injury involving damage to, for instance, your back, groin, hamstrings or knee, your sports therapist or physiotherapist will probably have given you some core stability exercises to do as part of your rehabilitation work. Within the repertoire of core stability there is a large range of exercises, the suitability of which will vary according to the injury and therapeutic needs of each individual.

There are three major groups of exercises:

- those focusing on getting the small deep-lying stabilising muscles (such as the lower abdominals and deep spinal muscles) to work properly. These exercises are often taken from clinical Pilates
- static bodyweight exercises that concentrate on developing stability and/or strength endurance in certain postures. These need you to learn how simultaneously to work your small stabiliser muscles and the larger mobiliser muscles. One popular example is the 'plank'
- traditional dynamic strength exercises for the main movement muscles of the trunk, often performed on the floor or Swiss ball.

While sports therapists use a variety of approaches, it is common to start you off working on the first type of exercise (how to use the smaller stability muscles properly) and then progress to more strength-based work as your injury improves.

Core stability work is by no means confined to the rehab clinic, however. Sports physicians, physiotherapists and strength and conditioning coaches also recommend that their clients perform regular core stability or trunk strength exercises to prevent injury. The rationale for prophylactic training is that increased recruitment of the stabiliser muscles and increased strength of the prime movers (main movement muscles) will carry over into better posture and more control, both in daily life and in sporting movements. So it is very likely you will have come across some core stability exercises through your local sports club, gym or any other general training context. Most of us tend to have a list of three or four of these exercises which we include in our workouts each week.

While this 'prehabilitative' strategy is well intentioned it has two limitations. The first is behavioural. Core stability exercises can quite quickly become 'bore stability'! It takes self-discipline to do 20 to 30 minutes of the same exercises three or more times a week over a long period, so most of us lapse, or at best skimp on this part of the workout after a while.

The second limitation is physiological. The key training principles of specificity and progression apply to core work in the same way that they do to any other aspect of physical fitness. In my experience it is quite common for an athlete to perform the same core routine over a long period and get very good at four or five movements or 'holds'. But teach the same athlete a new core exercise and they will find it difficult, simply because it's a new stimulus. The message is that progression and variety are key to optimising benefits of a strengthening programme.

The scheme of core training menus presented here aims to overcome the problems of non-compliance and lack of challenge, in order to provide a system where an individual can follow a prophylactic or rehabilitative core stability and strengthening programme using a wide variety of movements to maximise adaptations for improvement, and which muscle groups are targeted for training.

The system is designed for those who have already developed some basic skill in using their all-important lower abdominal stability muscles (transversus abdominis) and who are familiar with a number of core exercises. This is a challenging programme, covering all the trunk and pelvic muscles, and running from basic recruitment to very advanced strength movements.

The training system contains ten exercise menus, each using a single piece of training apparatus. A menu contains three to four exercises, which between them target most trunk and pelvic muscles. Some of the exercises involve resistance, some bodyweight, some are simply about muscle recruitment. Within a menu the difficulty of exercises varies; a couple of the menus are very advanced (and therefore not within the competence of all readers). Coaches, therapists and individuals should set the number of sets and repetitions for each exercise according to the normal principles of training fatigue and overload. If you are in doubt about how many sets and reps you should be performing, consult a qualified trainer or (if recovering from injury) a sports therapist, so that you are not working pointlessly or, worse, unsafely.

Select the most appropriate menus, and then use them in rotation. If you are using eight menus and doing four units of core training per week, over the course of a fortnight you will perform each menu once. This will ensure that you work all the muscles in a variety of ways, using different pieces of equipment.

Progressive overload: what it means

Progressive overload is one of the key principles of training. You start off exercising at a low and manageable level. Providing you allow enough time between sessions for recovery, this initial training dosage will produce a training response. After a certain time your body adapts, so you can then increase the dosage to produce further increases in fitness. If there is no progression then your fitness level will plateau.

Table 1: Example of a progressive overload programme

Week:	1 and 2	3 and 4	5 and 6	7 and 8
Reps & sets	2 sets x 5 reps	3 sets x 5 reps	3 sets x 8 reps	3 sets x 10 reps
Frequency	2 x per week	2 x per week	2 x per week	2 x per week

Table 1 shows a simple volume progression. The goal at the start is to learn the exercises correctly. In this example, you perform only 2 sets x 5 reps twice a week for weeks 1 and 2, to ensure the muscles and tendons involved in the exercise are not overloaded too much, too soon.

During weeks 3 and 4 you complete 50 per cent more reps by adding another set (3 x 5). Over the next 4 weeks, you build up to 3 sets x 10 reps, which is three times the original dosage. In this case the progressive schedule has targeted 'strength endurance', which is why the emphasis is on building up the number of repetitions over time rather than increasing the amount of weight.

Strength endurance training

Strength endurance aims to increase a muscle's ability to withstand repetitive forces or to be able to maintain its function for sustained periods. **Table 2** gives guidelines for developing strength endurance.

Table 2: Guidelines for developing strength endurance

Repetitions	10 to 20 *or* 10sec to 90sec holds per set (for static positions)
Sets	2 to 4
Intensity	At a resistance (weight) that results in fatigue during last few reps of each set
Rest	30 to 60 seconds between sets
Frequency	2 to 5 x per week
Phase duration	4 to 8 weeks

It will take 4 to 8 weeks to develop a significant improvement in strength endurance. At the start choose an appropriate resistance or, if it is a bodyweight movement, an appropriate level of position. Once you can do 20 reps (or 90sec holds of a static exercise), it is probably more effective to increase the resistance. Beyond about 20 reps the load has become too low to enable you to continue to develop your strength endurance, so to make the exercise more challenging, greater resistance (more weight) is needed.

'This is a challenging programme, covering all the trunk and pelvic muscles, and running from basic recruitment to very advanced strength movements'

Strength training

For strength training the resistance must be tough enough to permit you to perform no more than 10 repetitions per set. Rest periods between sets should be longer: 2 to 3 minutes to allow for the necessary recovery, and the weights should be progressively increased rather than upping the number of repetitions.

In general, if you are targeting strength improvements, Table 3 gives guidelines for effective progressions.

Table 3: Guidelines for developing strength

Repetitions	3 to 10
Sets	2 to 5
Intensity	Heavy weights to produce fatigue within each set
Rest	2 to 3 minutes between sets
Frequency	2 to 3 x per week
Phase duration	4 to 8 weeks

It is important not to overload the muscles and tendons too much, too soon, which is why you should start with lighter loads and more reps, and progress to heavier loads and fewer reps. By increasing the number of sets you can maintain volume when the reps decrease (starting, for instance, with 2 sets x 10 reps and progressing to 4 sets x 5 reps).

Menu 1: Floor, static

Menu rationale
To develop a basic level of lumbar and pelvic stability, working front, rear and side muscles of the trunk. This menu can also be used as a maintenance dose of training for intermediate to advanced level athletes.

The Plank

Overview: A common exercise that requires good abdominal strength and co-contraction of the abdominal wall musculature to hold the lumbar spine and pelvis in correct alignment.

Level: Basic/intermediate

Muscles targeted:
Rectus abdominis
Abdominal wall (transversus abdominis/internal obliques)

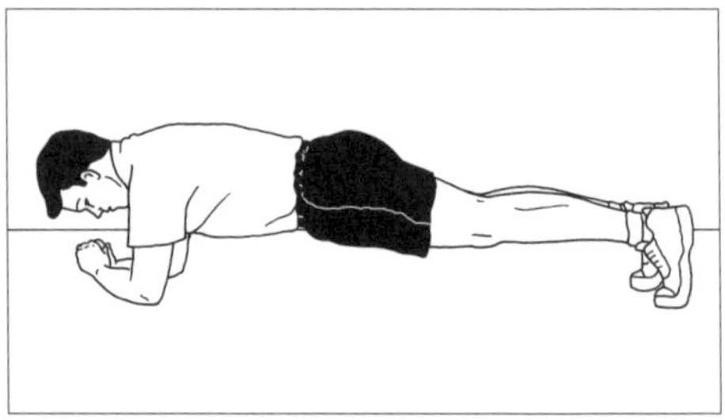

Technique: Hold a straight body position, supported on elbows and toes. Brace the abs, and set the low back in the neutral position, once you are up. Sometimes this requires a pelvic tilt to find the right position. The aim is to hold this position, keeping the upper spine extended, for an increasing length of time up to a maximum of 60 secs. Perform 2 to 3 sets. Keep shoulders back and chest out while maintaining the neutral lumbar position. This makes the exercise considerably more challenging.

Progression: Lift one leg just off the floor; hold the position without tilting at the pelvis.

The Side Plank

Overview: Recommended as a safe and effective exercise for the obliques and quadratus lumborum (a key lumbar stabilising muscle). Recent research also shows this to be an excellent exercise for the lower abdominal muscles.

Level: Basic/intermediate

Muscles targeted:
Obliques (internal and external)
Quadratus lumborum
Transversus abdominis

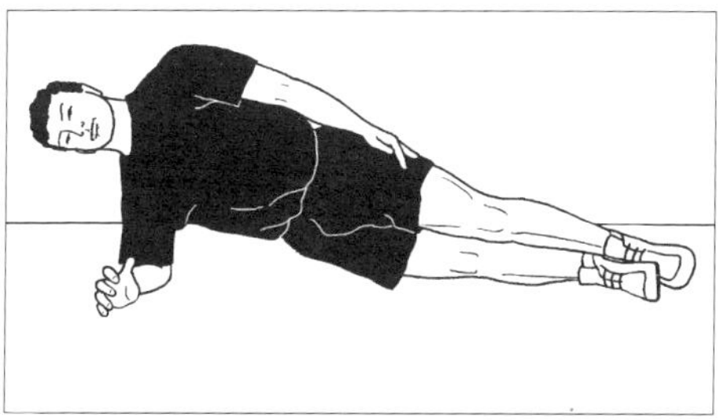

Technique: Lie on one side, ensuring the top hip is 'stacked' above the bottom hip. Push up until there is a straight bodyline through, feet, hips and head. Hold the position, increasing the length of hold up to a maximum of 60 secs. Perform 2 to 3 sets. Keep the elbow under the shoulder to avoid upper body strain. Lower under control and repeat on opposite side.

Progression: Raise the top leg in the air and hold it in that position throughout.

The Gluteal Bridge

Overview: Research suggests this is more a low-back than gluteal exercise. However, it is a good way to learn how to recruit the gluteals (buttock muscles) in the 'inner range' position.

Level : Basic

Muscles targeted:
Gluteus maximus
Erector spinae/multifidus

Technique: Lie on the floor with your knees bent. Squeeze your gluteals and then push your hips up until there is a straight line through knee and hip to upper body. Shoulders remain on the floor. Beware of raising too high or of flaring the ribs, which pushes the back into hyperextension. Hold the position. Start with 5 sets of 10 sec holds, progressing to 2 to 3 sets of 60 sec holds.

Progression:
Extend one leg carefully ahead of you, and hold the position without dropping or tilting the pelvis.

'Birddog' or 'Superman'

Overview: Recommended as a safe and effective exercise for the lumbar and thoracic portions of the erector spinae (long back) muscle. This exercise also requires co-contraction of the abdominal wall muscles to stabilise the pelvis.

Level: Basic/intermediate

Muscles targeted:
Thoracic and lumbar portions of erector spinae

Technique: Start with hands below shoulders and knees below hips. Set your low back into neutral and brace your abs slightly. Slowly slide back one leg and slide forward the opposite arm. Ensure that the back does not slip into extension, and that the shoulders and pelvis do not tilt sideways. Hold, increasing the duration up to a maximum of 20 secs. Slowly bring your leg and arm back and swap sides. Perform sets of 5 to 10, alternating sides after each hold.

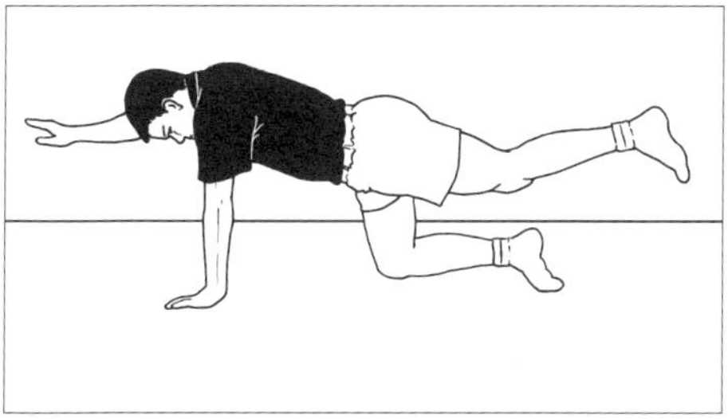

Progression: none.

Menu 2: Floor, dynamic

Menu rationale
To develop a good level of strength endurance in the major trunk muscles. Overall the level of these exercises is intermediate to advanced.

Active Straight Leg Raise

Overview: Requires a strong static contraction of the abdominals to stabilise the lumbar spine against the load of the legs. It also requires good active range of motion of the hamstrings.

Level: intermediate/advanced

Muscles targeted:
Rectus abdominis
Abdominal wall
Hip flexors

Technique: Lie on your back with knees bent. Set your lumbar spine in neutral and brace the abs. Lift one leg up straight in the air, ensure your back does not move. Lift the other leg up, again keeping your back in place. (If the back cannot be stabilised during this movement, the exercise is too advanced, and more static transversus stability control work will be needed first.)

Keeping one leg in the air, slowly lower the other down to the floor. Only go as far as you can, until you feel the lumbar spine start to move. Placing your fingers under your back will help you to gauge when this happens. Keep bracing the abs and then lift the leg slowly back up. Repeat with the other leg. Perform sets of 5 to 10 reps, alternating legs.

Progression: Lower and raise both legs together

Oblique Crunch

Overview: A good exercise for both the obliques and the abdominals.

Level: Intermediate

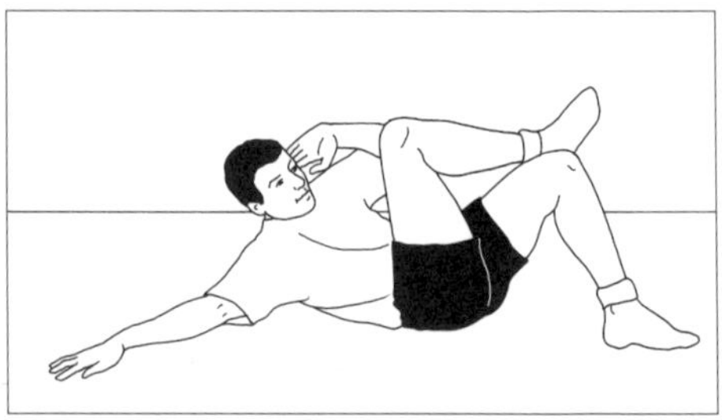

Muscles targeted:
Rectus abdominis
Obliques

Technique: Lie on your back with right ankle resting on left knee. Right arm is placed on the floor out to the side. Keeping the right shoulder down, curl the left shoulder up to the right knee. Crunch at the top and return slowly, under control. Perform sets of 15 to 30 reps on each side in turn. Avoid 'head nodding' during the movement: keep head off the floor and look forward throughout.

Progression: Hold a dumb-bell in the hand by your head. Keep arm still so you are forced to raise the dumbell using your abs and not your arm.

Side Lying Hip Abduction

Overview: This is an exercise to isolate the use of gluteus medius (upper buttock). Strength in this muscle group has been shown to be useful in preventing lower limb injuries in female athletes, and see Sean Fyfe *(p41)* for further discussion.

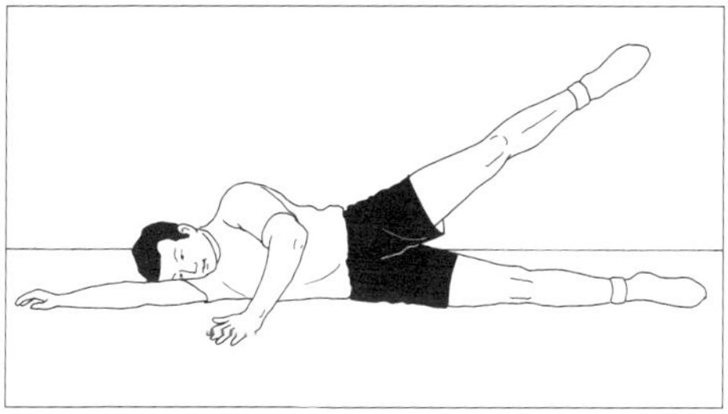

Level: Basic

Muscles targeted:
Gluteus medius

Technique: Lie on your side and set pelvis so your top hip is stacked above lower hip. Roll shoulders forward a little and brace the abs to control pelvic position. Lift the top leg slowly up and down, without hitching at the hip. Perform sets of 20 to 30 reps, each side in turn.

Progression: Weight the top leg with an ankle weight or tie a resistance band between your ankles and pull the band apart as you lift the leg.

Lying Windscreen Wipers

Overview: An advanced active mobility exercise working the obliques and trunk rotation.

Level: Advanced

Muscles targeted:
Rectus abdominis
Obliques

Technique: Lie on your back with arms out to the sides. Lift legs straight up in the air until the hip is at 90 degrees. Set the lumbar spine in neutral and aim to keep it set throughout. Keeping legs straight and maintaining hip angle, move the legs to one side, controlling any movement in the trunk. Go as far as you can in control, keeping your upper back and shoulders on the floor. Bring the legs to a halt, pull them back up to the start position and then over to the other side, under control. The slow side-to-side movement is like a 'windscreen wiper' arc.

Menu 3: Swiss ball, static

The four exercises in this routine challenge your ability to hold good posture and pelvic alignment against both bodyweight and the instability of the Swiss ball. The positions of the holds are similar to the static floor exercises in Menu 1, except that they are performed on the ball. Research shows that the performance of core exercises upon the labile surface of the Swiss ball can increase the levels of trunk muscle activation; so this menu is a progression from floor-based work. *(See p23 for my more in-depth consideration of the value of working with Swiss balls.)* Overall Menu 3 is intermediate in difficulty.

Swiss Ball Sit and Leg Lift

Overview: Challenges your ability to co-contract the abdominal wall and maintain a neutral lumbar spine position on an unstable seat.

Level: Basic

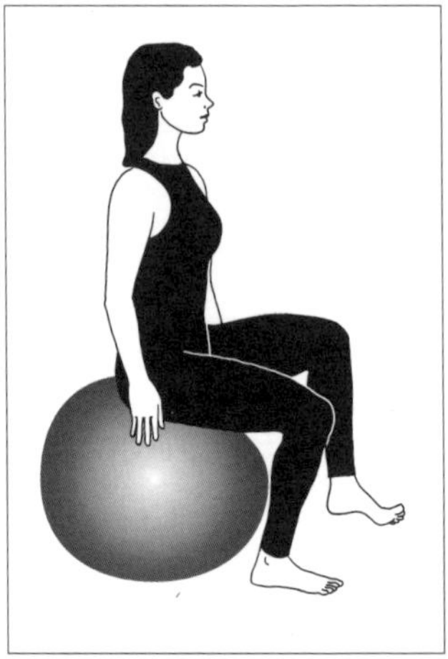

Muscles targeted:
Abdominal wall
(transversus abdominis,
internal obliques)

Technique: Sit on a Swiss ball with hips on the top of the ball and feet hip-width apart. Ensure the size of ball is correct: your knees should be level with or slightly lower than your hips and at 90 degrees in sitting.

Relax and find a neutral lumbar spine position. Set this position by lightly bracing your abdominal muscles. Think about good upper back and shoulder posture as you sit (stomach in, chest lifted, shoulders low and relaxed). It is important to hold an upright sitting position – not leaning forward or back.

Once you are set, carefully lift one foot a few centimetres off the floor. Maintain your balance, lumbar and pelvic alignments as you hold the position on one leg.

Hold for a count of 5 to 10, maintaining form. Perform 5 reps each side.

Progression: Keeping the lifted foot only just off the floor, straighten the leg in front of you, stretching the hamstring. Resist any tilting of your pelvis as the leg straightens by keeping a good hold of the abdominals and maintaining posture against the stretch.

Supine Swiss Ball Bridge

Overview: A posterior-chain exercise (hamstrings, gluteals and back), where the aim is to hold perfectly straight hip and back alignment against the load of your bodyweight and the instability of the ball. A big co-contraction of the trunk muscles is required to perform this exercise well.

Level: Intermediate

Muscles targeted:
Gluteals
Hamstrings
Erector spinae
Abdominals
Obliques

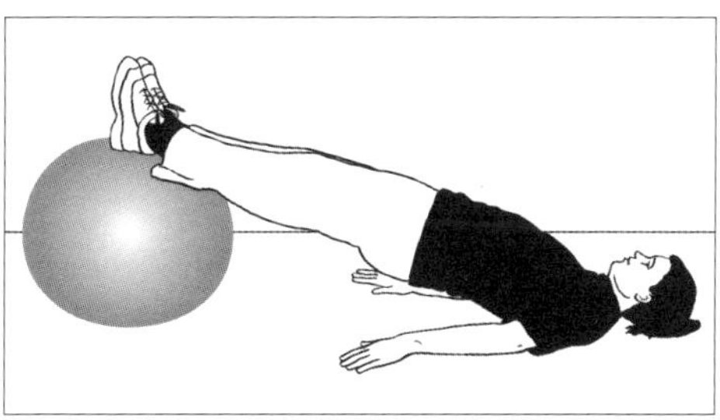

Technique: Lie on your back with heels on the top of the Swiss ball, hip-width apart to aid stability. Suck in the abs and squeeze up from your gluteals, lifting your hips until there is a straight line from heels to upper back. Shoulders and head stay firmly on the floor. Take care not to lift the hips too high or flare the ribs so that your back hyperextends.

Hold for 30 seconds and lower under control. Perform 2 to 3 sets.

Progression:
i. Place the feet close together on the ball to increase the balance challenge as you lift your hips.
ii. Roll your legs slowly from side to side with control, keeping hips up for an advanced level of challenge.

Swiss Ball Gluteal Bridge

Overview: A second posterior-chain exercise. But with the knees bent and the weight bearing down through the feet, the work is felt mainly in the gluteal muscles

Level: Intermediate

Muscles targeted:
Gluteals
Erector spinae
Abdominals
Obliques

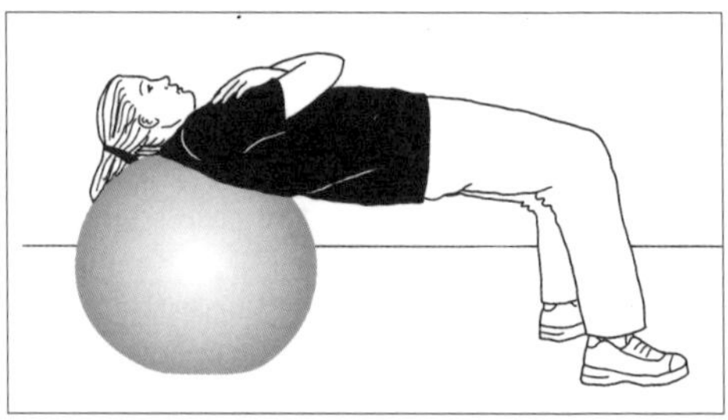

Technique: Lie on your back with your shoulders and head on the top of a Swiss ball; feet on the ground, hip-width apart for stability.

Squeezing up from the gluteals, lift hips until there is a straight line running through the knees, hips and shoulders. Do not lift the hips too high or flare the ribs so that your back hyperextends.

Hold for 30 seconds and lower under control. Perform 2 to 3 sets.

Progression:
i. Place the feet close together to increase the balance challenge.
ii. Single-leg bridge, alternating legs with 5 second holds, is an advanced challenge.

Swiss Ball Plank

Overview: A challenging strength exercise for abdominals, focusing on maintaining good alignment of the spine.

Level: Intermediate to advanced

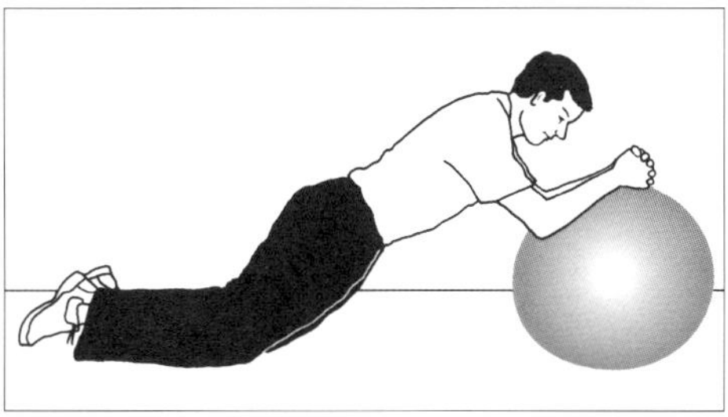

Muscles targeted: Abdominals

Technique: Kneel in front of the Swiss ball and place elbows on the top of the ball in the centre. Slowly roll the ball away from your body until there is a straight line through knees, hips and head and your weight is being supported through your elbows down on to the ball.

Once in this position it may be necessary to tilt the pelvis so that it is held in neutral with correct lumbar spine alignment. Also be careful not to round off the shoulders: aim for a 'long spine'. The better your spinal alignment, the harder the work for the abdominals. If the main pressure is felt in the low back, either your alignment is incorrect or you have insufficient abdominal strength-endurance to hold the correct line.

Hold at the far point for 30 to 60 secs with good form. Perform 2 to 3 sets.

Progression: Move the ball around, forward, left and right with your upper body whilst keeping your hips in place and your head still in its alignment.

Menu 4: Swiss ball, dynamic

These exercises challenge trunk strength. The use of the Swiss ball both increases the difficulty because of the instability, and allows you to work through useful ranges of movement. This menu targets the front, back and side of the trunk musculature at intermediate to advanced level.

Swiss Ball Back Extension

Overview: The use of the ball for this exercise allows the movement to isolate back extension without hip extension; and to co-ordinate upper back extension with lumbar extension.

Level: Intermediate

Muscles targeted:
Erector spinae (lumbar and thoracic portions)

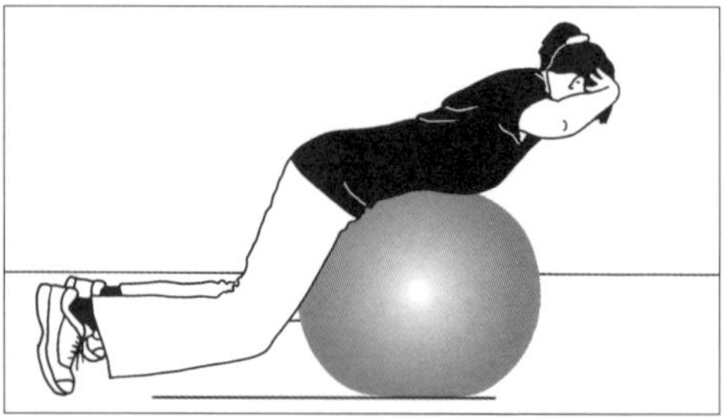

Technique: Kneel over a Swiss ball with thighs and stomach in contact with the ball and head and shoulders dipping over the front of the ball. With your back straight and parallel to the floor, position the lumbar spine in neutral and then set your hips so they do not move.

Allow the chest to drop and fall over the ball, flexing the upper back. Place your hands at the sides of the head, elbows bent. From this position, lift your chest up, extending your upper back until it is higher than at the starting position. Maintain abdominal contraction throughout to fix the hips and limit hyperextension of the lumbar spine.

Perform 10 reps under control, increasing to 20 reps; 2 to 3 sets.

Progression: Add a light dumb-bell held behind the head for extra resistance.

Swiss Ball Overhead Pulls

Overview: The use of the ball for this exercise allows full extension of the body. The abdominals have to work hard to support the spine as the arms extend and pull back. Very good for shoulder stability.

Level: Intermediate to advanced

Muscles targeted:
Abdominals
Latissimus dorsi
Pectorals
Scapular stability muscles

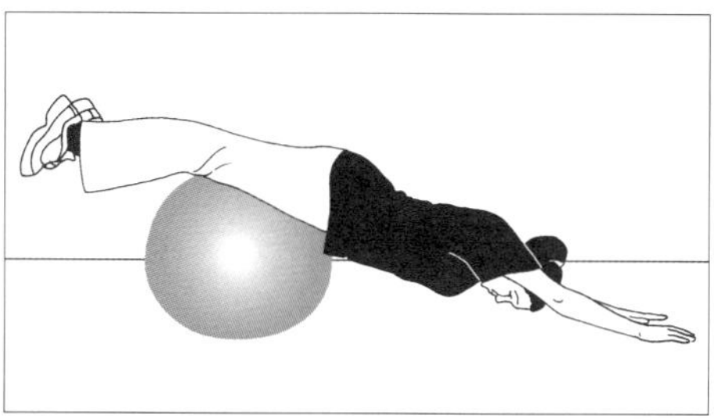

Technique: Start in the press-up position with your shins on the ball and hands shoulder width apart under shoulders. Place knees apart slightly for stability. Set lumbar spine in neutral and ensure that the shoulders are stable with shoulder blades down and chest out.

Roll backwards until your hands are above your head, maintaining straight body position and neutral low back. Use your abs, ensuring your hips do not drop. Brace your abs and pull yourself forwards to return to the start position.

Perform 5 reps with good form, increasing to 10 reps; 2 to 3 sets.

Progression: Lengthen your bridge position by starting with feet alone on the ball. The abs have to support more bodyweight.

Swiss Ball Squat Thrust

Overview: The old-school exercise transposed to the ball. This allows for a focus on the flexion of the hips and low back, maximising the use of abs. Holding the position through several reps is a great strength-endurance challenge for the abdominals. Unlike the traditional version where speed is of the essence, the Swiss ball version is more demanding if performed slowly with control.

Level: Intermediate

Muscles targeted: Abdominals

Technique: Start in the press-up position with shins on the ball, hands shoulder-width apart under the shoulders. Place knees slightly apart for stability. Set lumbar spine in neutral and ensure shoulders are stable with shoulder blades down and chest out.

Pull knees to your chest and crunch the abs to get an extra flex of the hips and back. Slowly extend knees back, using your abs to prevent the hips dropping down.

Perform 10 reps slowly, increasing to 20 reps; 2 to 3 sets.

Progression: Perform the squat thrust and the overhead pull as a combination exercise.

Swiss Ball Side Crunch

Overview: An excellent exercise for the obliques. The Swiss ball simply replaces the need for a frame or partner support for your legs. Electromyography research has shown this exercise delivers high recruitment levels of the obliques.

Level: Intermediate

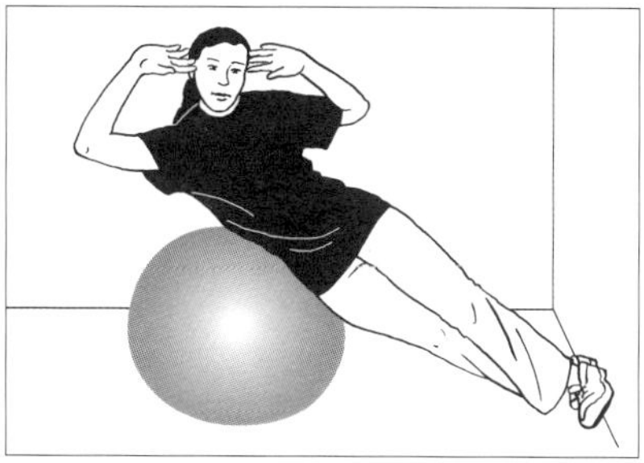

Muscles targeted:
Obliques

Technique: Position yourself sideways on the ball, balanced on lower hip with top hip stacked vertically. Brace feet against a wall, one slightly in front of the other for stability. Ensure a straight line through legs, hips and shoulders. Place your hands, elbows bent, by your head.

Lift upper body up away from the ball, crunching sideways towards your feet and focusing upon your oblique muscles. Slowly return, under control.

Perform 10 reps, increasing to 20 reps; 2 to 3 sets.

Progression: Hold a weight across your chest to increase the load.

Menu 5: Pulley, kneeling

Bodyweight-only exercises by definition have strict limits on your ability to increase the load against which the muscles are working. So the main tool for progression is to increase the number of sets and reps being performed, which is good for muscular endurance, but not for pure strength.

The pulley system allows us to treat trunk training like limb training, working at higher resistance levels as your strength improves. Overall, these exercises are advanced.

Chop Rotation

Overview: Excellent for dynamic trunk rotation strength co-ordinated with the upper body. This exercise and its pair *(see overleaf)* are functional to many sporting and daily life movements. When performed in the kneeling position, the exercise requires dissociation between the pelvis and shoulder rotation, which is a great stability challenge.

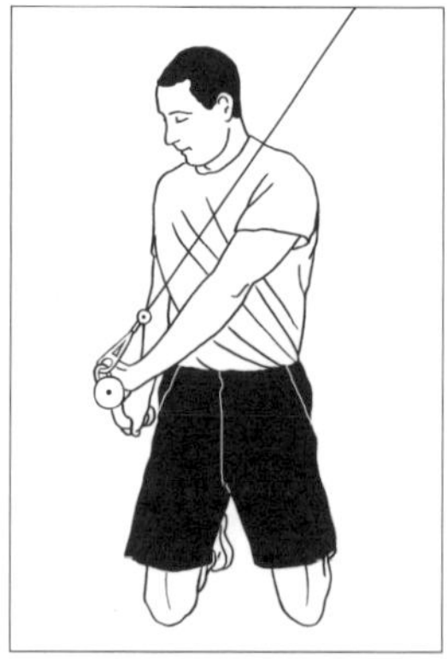

Level: Advanced

Muscles targeted:
Abdominals
Obliques
(Plus upper body)

Technique: Kneel, facing forwards, by the side of the pulley column. Handle attachment is set at (standing) head height. Fix the hips square to the front and set your lumbar spine in neutral. Twisting through the waist, turn shoulders towards the pulley column and grasp the handle with both hands. Pull down on the handle, rotating your shoulders away from the column and crunching down. Finish with hands by your hips and shoulders facing away. Hips remain square to the front throughout the movement.

Perform 8 to 10 reps; 2 to 3 sets each side.

Progression: Increase the weight, keeping to sets of 8 to 10 reps.

Lift Rotation

Overview: The natural opposite to the chop movement exercise. Perform these two as a pair to ensure balanced development of trunk rotation strength. The lift movement requires co-contraction of the low back muscles with the obliques to produce the rotation.

Level: Advanced

Muscles targeted:
Erector spinae
Obliques
(Plus upper body)

Technique: Kneel, facing forwards, by the side of the pulley column. Handle attachment is set just below (kneeling) hip height. Fix hips square to the front and set your lumbar spine in neutral. Twisting through the waist, turn shoulders towards the pulley column and grasp the handle with both hands. Pull up on the handle, rotating the shoulders away. Finish with hands above your head and shoulders facing away from the column. Hips remain square to the front throughout.

Perform 8 to 10 reps; 2 to 3 sets each side.

Progression: Increase the weight, keeping to sets of 8 to 10 reps.

Pulley Crunch

Overview: This is a pure trunk flexion movement targeting the development of abdominal strength. The use of the weights allows for high resistances. Care must be taken to fix the hips throughout the exercise, otherwise the hip flexors will contribute, significantly reducing the training effect on the abdominals.

Level: Advanced

Muscles targeted:
Abdominals

Technique: Kneel with back to the pulley column, holding a rope attachment with each hand around your neck. Start with hips fully extended (ie, kneeling fully upright) and pelvis set in neutral. Shoulders, hips and knees should all be in line and upright.

Focusing on the abs, crunch down, pulling the weight and flexing your trunk forward. The arms simply hold on – avoid using them to assist in pulling the weight. Ensure the pelvis remains set and stable throughout: all the movement comes from the spine flexion, so there should be no hip flexion, forward lean or forwards pelvic tilt.

Perform 5 to 10 reps; 2 to 3 sets.

Progression: Increase the weight, keeping to sets of 5 to 10 reps.

Menu 6: Pulley, standing

This menu challenges pelvic stability during unilateral standing upper body movements. The kinds of arm movements undertaken in many sports create strong rotational forces that have to be controlled by the trunk and pelvic muscles. The aim of these exercises, therefore, is to develop co-ordination and control of the pelvis.

Research has shown that unilateral exercises increase the recruitment of the core musculature. The core and pelvic muscles will all be using static contractions to hold the required postures, while the upper body muscles will be producing the limb movements. The resistance load on the arm is secondary to the stability challenge of the core. Overall this menu is intermediate.

Rear Sling

Overview: The challenge of this exercise and its pair *(see opposite)* is to establish perfect pelvic alignment, while standing on one leg, against a rotational force from the upper body.

Level: Intermediate

Muscles targeted:
Abdominal wall
Adductors
Gluteus medius
(Deltoid and rotator cuff)

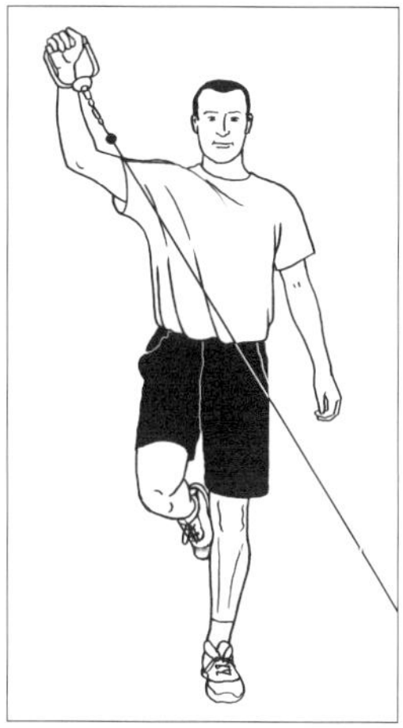

Technique: Stand on one leg to the side of the pulley column. Handle is attached at below-hip height. Grasp the handle with the hand on the opposite side (opposite to standing leg). Set perfect posture and pelvic alignment.

Brace the core and then pull the weight up and around the body, keeping the elbow straight, so that the arm rotates up and out. Finish with hand above your head and out to the side slightly. The aim is to maintain perfect balance and pelvic alignment as you raise and lower the arm diagonally. Reposition to repeat exercise for opposite leg/arm.

Perform 10 reps each side increasing to 20 reps; 2 to 3 sets.

Progression: Increase the weight.

Front Sling

Overview: This is the natural opposite of the rear sling exercise. It involves a forward arm rotation, which must be controlled.

Level: Intermediate

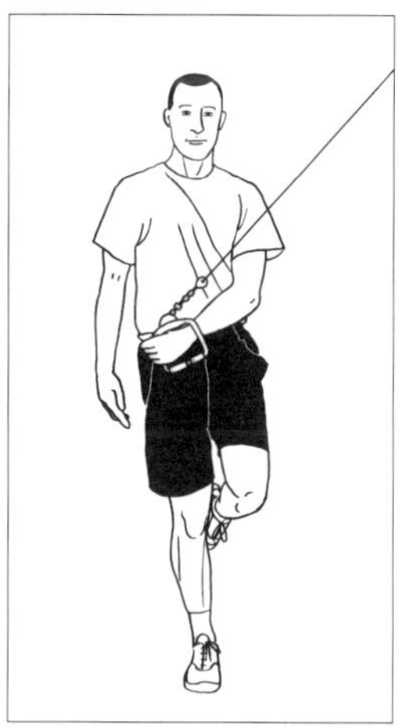

Muscles targeted:
Abdominal wall
Adductors
Gluteus medius
(Pectorals and rotator cuff)

Technique: Stand on one leg to the side of pulley column. Handle is attached at above shoulder height. Grasp the handle with the arm nearest the column (opposite side to standing leg). Set perfect posture and pelvic alignment.

Brace your core; pull the weight down and around the body, keeping the elbow straight so that the arm rotates down and round. Finish with hand next to your hip across your body. The aim is to maintain perfect balance and pelvic alignment as you lower and raise the arm. Reposition to repeat with opposite leg/arm.

Perform 10 reps each side, increasing to 20 reps; 2 to 3 sets.

Progression: Increase the weight.

One Leg, One Arm Rowing

Overview: The challenge of this exercise is to maintain stability while standing on one leg and controlling against a pulling force from the upper body. The pelvis must stay fixed when the upper back and shoulder are pulling backwards.

Level: Intermediate

Muscles targeted:
Abdominal wall
Adductors
Gluteus medius
(Rear deltoid, rhomboids, latissimus dorsi)

Technique: Stand on one leg, facing the pulley column. Handle is attached at waist height. Grasp the handle with the opposite arm (same side as lifted leg). Your hand will be out directly in front of you in the start position. Set perfect posture and pelvic alignment, standing tall with shoulders back.

Brace your core; pull on the cable, leading with the elbow in a rowing movement Finish with hand by your side and elbow behind you. The aim is to maintain perfect balance and pelvic alignment as you perform the rowing movement. Reposition to repeat with opposite leg/arm.

Perform 10 reps each side; 2 to 3 sets.

Progression: Increase the weight.

Menu 7: Medicine ball, floor

The four exercises in this menu all involve throwing and catching the medicine ball while performing a trunk flexion or rotation movement. The action of throwing the ball during the muscle-shortening phase of each of the exercises increases the force production of the trunk muscles. The action of catching the ball at the start or during the muscle-lengthening phase of each exercise not only increases the force production but also the overall stability challenge.

The impact that the catch has on the upper limb has to be controlled by the trunk. You should be aiming to maintain good spine alignment and correct movement while making the catch. Only use a weight of medicine ball that will allow you to perform the exercises with good technique. If the ball is too heavy, you will sacrifice core stability, irrespective of your arm strength.

Overall these exercises are advanced. However they are also safe and effective for young athletes using light medicine balls to develop dynamic trunk movement and control.

Sit Up and Throw

Overview: An advanced version of a sit-up exercise, in which the throwing action makes the crunch phase faster and the catching action adds load to the return phase.

Level: Advanced

Muscles targeted:
Abdominals
(Plus upper body)

Technique: You will need a partner to receive and pass the ball. Alternatively perform the exercise in front of a wall and use a medicine ball that will bounce back.

Start in the sit-up position (knees bent) with hands up ready to receive the ball. Catch the ball and begin to lower back down. Do not collapse back down, control it with the abs and keep hands above the head as you lower down.

Once shoulders are touching the floor (keeping head up and eyes forward), reverse the movement. Throw the ball forward and crunch up at the same time. Follow the throwing action and complete the sit-up as fast as possible. Make sure you crunch as you throw so that the abs contribute to the force of the throw and help you sit up faster. Men should start with a 5kg ball; women with a 3kg ball.

Perform 10 to 20 reps; 2 to 3 sets

Progression: Progress to heavier ball once 3 sets of 20 reps is comfortable

45-degree Sit, Catch and Pass

Overview: A very tough stability exercise that requires massive trunk musculature co-contraction to hold a good spine alignment against the impact of making the catch.

Level: Advanced

Muscles targeted:
Erector spinae
Abdominals
Obliques

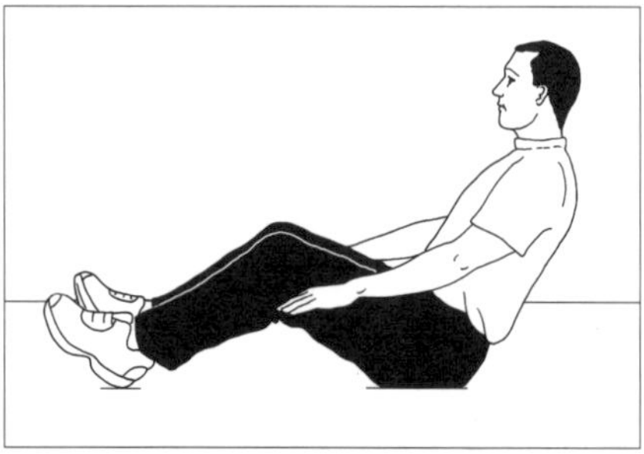

Technique: Sit up with knees bent and lean back at 45 degrees. Aim to hold a 'lengthened' spine, with lumbar spine in neutral, shoulders back and neck long and relaxed. It takes a fair amount of control and strength endurance simply to hold this posture perfectly. Aim to get this right before progressing on to the catch and pass.

Raise hands in front of your face and receive a pass from a partner, around this height. As you catch the ball you must hold the long spine position. Do not flex the low back, or become round-shouldered. Gently throw the ball back. Men should start with a 3kg ball; women with a 2kg ball.

Complete a few passes, holding the position for 30 seconds. Perform 2 to 3 sets.

Progression: Raising the hands to above head height makes the stability challenge of the catch significantly harder. Catches made to either side of the head are also more challenging.

Sit and Twist Pass

Overview: A trunk rotation exercise involving catching and passing the medicine ball, which provides a challenge to the obliques to produce powerful rotation, but also pelvic stability, so that the sitting position is stable throughout the movement.

Level: Advanced

Muscles targeted:
Abdominals
Obliques

Technique: Sit up with knees bent and lean back at 45 degrees. Aim to hold a 'lengthened' spine, with lumbar spine in neutral, shoulders back and neck long and relaxed. Your feet, knees and hips should remain reasonably still throughout this exercise, the rotation coming from your waist and not your hips.

Hold hands to one side ready to receive the ball. Catch the ball to one side and absorb the catch by turning your shoulders further to that side. Reverse the rotation, turning back to the middle and release the ball. Continue rotating to the other side; receive the ball the other side and continue. Ensure you can hold good posture throughout the movement, with a long spine and wide shoulders. Men should start with a 4 to 5kg ball; women with a 2 to 3kg ball.

Perform 10 to 20 reps.

Progression: Increase the weight of the ball once you can perform a set of 20 reps comfortably with perfect technique.

Kneeling Twist Pass

Overview: To perform the rotation movement in this position demands a greater range of motion, helping to develop strength through the full range of trunk rotation. It may also help to develop trunk rotation range of movement.

Level: Intermediate to advanced

Muscles targeted:
Obliques

Technique: Kneel upright with good posture (lumbar spine in neutral, chest out, shoulders low). Start with the ball in hands and twist shoulders and head round as far as you can. Then, under control, twist around to the other side as far as possible, and hand the ball to partner. Turn back to the start position, receive the ball again and continue.

The aim of the movement is to rotate through the biggest shoulder turn you have. You can allow the hips to rotate a little with the shoulders, but not too much. You should feel a stretch in the side at the end of each twist.

As you gain greater flexibility and stability you will be able to fix your pelvis square to the front and rotate through an increasingly full range of motion. Men should start with a 5 to 6kg ball; women with a 3 to 4kg ball.

Perform 10 reps then take the ball to the opposite side and repeat.

Menu 8: Medicine ball, standing

The aim of this menu is to perform trunk movements while standing on one leg. This is functional training for balance in sports and daily living activities. These exercises are advanced because of the requirements for lower limb balance and body movement awareness, which makes controlled performance of these trunk movements quite difficult. These moves also use the hip rotator and abductor muscles for control and stability.

One-leg Twist Pass

Overview: A trunk rotation exercise performed on one leg. This requires good pelvic stability at the hip of the standing leg, for the trunk rotation to be dissociated from the pelvis.

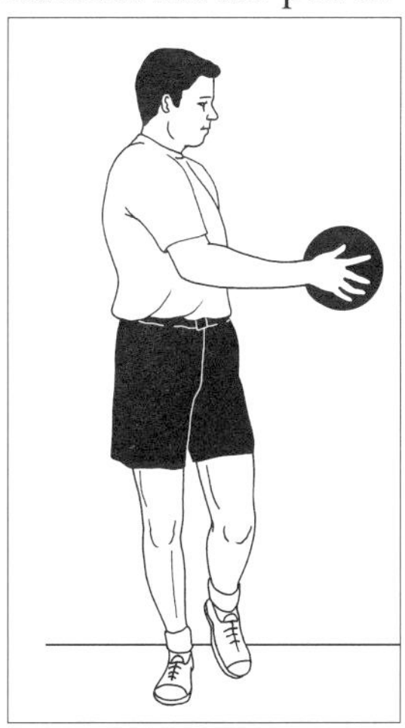

Level: Advanced

Muscles targeted:
Gluteus medius
Piriformis
Abdominal wall
Obliques

Technique: Stand on one leg with hips facing square to the front. Hold medicine ball slightly out in front. Slowly twist from side to side. The rotation comes from the waist only, head turning with the shoulders. Keep pelvis fixed square and knee in line with second toe throughout. Men should start with a 5 to 6kg ball; women with a 3 to 4kg ball.

Perform 10 slow reps; 2 to 3 sets. Repeat on other leg.

Progression: Swap the ball for a pulley machine and add resistance, once you have mastered the controlled balance on one leg.

One-leg Deadlifts with Rotation

Overview: An advanced exercise for the posterior chain of muscles, which includes rotation to challenge control of pelvis.

Level: Advanced

Muscles targeted:
Erector spinae
Gluteals (max and med)
Hamstrings
Piriformis

Technique: Stand on one leg. Flex the free leg a little at the knee to lift it off the floor, but do not flex or extend the hip of the free leg throughout the movement, in order to keep pelvis in control. Hold the ball in front of you.

Bend down, flexing at the knee and the hip. Lower down until the ball touches the floor by your foot, all the time keeping your arms straight and without reaching excessively with your upper back (ie, maintain a reasonably flat back). Stand back up, pushing down through the foot to use your gluteals correctly to extend the hips.

Alternate between touching the ball down on the inside and then the outside of the standing foot. This means you are internally or externally rotating the hip on alternate repetitions, challenging control of hip rotation. Keep the knee in line with second toe as much as possible throughout. Men should use a 5kg ball; women use a 3kg ball.

Start with 5 slow controlled reps, 2 to 3 sets. Build up to 10 reps. Repeat on the opposite leg.

Progression: Increase the weight of the ball or use a dumb-bell as you get stronger.

One-leg Catch and Pass

Overview: The main aim of this exercise is to control the impact of the catch without losing balance or rotating excessively at the hips. It's all about how effectively you can anticipate the impact and produce the required stiffness throughout the body to retain good posture and control. This is a very useful 'reaction'-type stability exercise.

Level: Advanced

Muscles targeted:
Everything

Technique: Stand on one leg with good posture (lumbar spine neutral, chest out, shoulders wide) and with hips square to the front. Hold hands up ready to catch. Receive catches anywhere within arm's reach. Make sure the passes are varied in their placement. Aim to restrict movement to arms and/or turning your shoulders, keeping the pelvis and lower limb stable. Use a 2 to 3kg ball that is not too big, so it is easy to catch.

Start with 30 sec bouts of catch and pass on each leg; 2 to 3 sets.

Progression: Receive more forceful passes so the impact of the catch is greater.

Menu 9: Resistance-based

Menu rationale
The aim of these three exercises is to progress the loading in order to build high-level trunk muscle strength. These exercises can be performed in the 5- to 10-repetition range with a suitably high weight for this number of reps. As you get stronger, you should prioritise an increase in weight rather than an increase in the number of reps. Overall, these exercises are very advanced.

Crunch with Weight

Overview: The standard isolated abdominal exercise with increased load.

Level: Advanced

Muscles targeted: Abdominals

Technique: Perform the crunch in the usual way: knees bent, low back flat, head up and looking forward. Curl the shoulders up and down using just the abdominals. The weight (medicine ball, dumb-bell or barbell weight plate) should be held above or behind the head. Arms are fixed, all they do is hold the weight in place. Do not use arms to move the weight relative to head as the crunch is performed. Keeping the elbows out helps to achieve this.

Perform 5 to10 reps; 2 to 3 sets.

Progression: Increase weight, maintaining the range of 5 to 10 reps per set.

Reverse Hypers

Overview: An excellent hip and back extension exercise to which it is very simple to add load.

Level: Advanced

Muscles targeted:
Erector spinae
Gluteals

Technique: Lie on your front on a horizontal bench, with hips just off the end of the bench. Grasp bench legs firmly for support. Your legs should be straight with a dumb-bell between the ankles for resistance. Squeezing the gluteals, extend hips and lift legs and the dumb-bell off the floor. Stop when your back is slightly hyper-extended and hips are fully extended. Lower slowly until feet are just off the floor and continue.

Perform 8 to 10 reps; 2 to 3 sets.

Progression: Increase weight, maintaining the range of 8 to 10 reps per set.

Reverse Crunch with Weight

Overview: This is a great exercise, as it requires good co-ordination and strength. Research shows that the obliques as well as the abdominals work very hard during this exercise, making it excellent value.

Level: Advanced

Muscles targeted:
Abdominals
Obliques

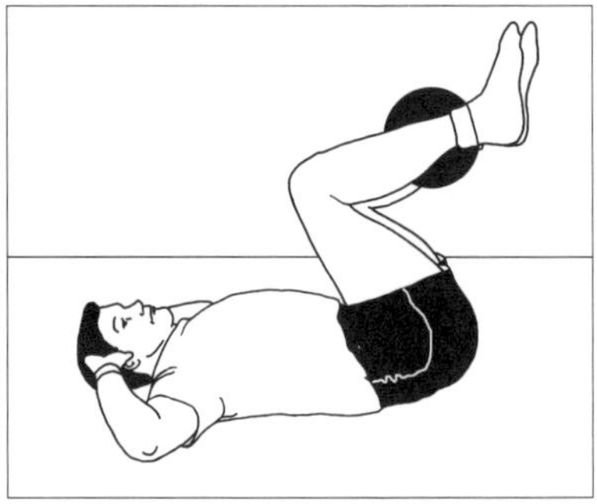

Technique: Lie on back with hands behind head and elbows out to the sides. Knees should be bent and heels close to bum. Hold weight between your legs. Initiate the movement by curling the pelvis upwards (flattening the back into the floor) and then continue to use the abs to pull the low back and pelvis off the floor. This is the bit that requires good co-ordination, as the temptation is to kick with the legs and pull the hips up with the hip flexors. Learn to focus on the abs before you add weight, as if you do this strictly it is very tough, especially for women (whose pelvises are relatively heavier).

Perform 5 to 10 reps; 2 to 3 sets.

Progression: Increase weight, maintaining the range of 5 to 10 reps per set.

Menu 10: Hanging Bar

Menu rationale

The aim of these three exercises is to work the abdominals as hard as possible with very advanced, gymnastic-style movements. Reasonable upper body strength is required for these exercises.

Hanging Leg Lifts

Overview: This exercise requires you to lift the full weight of your legs and (if possible) your pelvis, while hanging from a bar. Anyone who can perform these movements well through a good range of motion has achieved good strength.

Level: Advanced

Muscles targeted:
Abdominals
Obliques
Hip flexors

Technique: Hang from a bar with arms straight. Lift knees, bringing them up as high as possible. At the top of the movement the knees should be near the chest and pelvis should be curled upwards (low back flexed). This extra curl of the pelvis ensures that the abdominals are working maximally. Do not kick legs up or swing the body excessively. Simply draw up knees, crunching as you lift. It is important to feel that the abdominals are doing the lion's share of the work rather than the hip flexors or front of thigh muscles.

Perform 5 to 10 reps;, 2 to 3 sets.

Progression: Perform the same exercise with straight legs, lifting them up to 90 degrees in front of you, curling the pelvis at the top of the movement.

Windscreen Wipers

Overview: The ultimate ab-buster. Anyone who can do 10 reps of this exercise with good technique has a very strong core!

Level: Super advanced

Muscles targeted:
Abdominals
Obliques
Hip flexors

Technique: Hang from bar with arms straight. Lift legs up in the air until feet are at approx head height. Maintaining the height of the lift, take the legs from side to side in an arc. The movement will look like a windscreen wiper, moving from side to side. Aim for at least 45 degrees of movement to each side.

Perform 5 to10 reps; 2 to 3 sets.

Progression: The straighter the legs, the harder the exercise. Increasing the range of movement to each side also makes it tougher.

Candlesticks

Overview: Another beauty! Lots of strength required to control this movement; only for the very strong.

Level: Super advanced

Muscles targeted:
Abdominals
Obliques
Hip flexors

Technique: Lie flat and raise yourself up to a shoulder stand position, holding on to a bench/table leg/partner's leg with your hands above your head. Establish a fully extended hip and leg position and then begin to lower your body down slowly to the floor. The body should move in an arc as a single unit (no sagging in the back, or bending at the hips or knees). Lower under control from vertical to just above horizontal.

Gripping firmly for stability, lift your body back up into shoulder stand, again keeping everything straight and aligned in a single unit.

Slow and controlled movement on the way down will help, and a maximal contraction of everything will get you back up.

Perform 3 to 5 reps; 2 to 3 sets.

Progression: I think that's tough enough.

Raphael Brandon

Authors' notes

Raphael Brandon MSc is a sports conditioning and fitness specialist, working as the London region strength and conditioning coach for the English Institute of Sport.

Sean Fyfe is a physiotherapist, tennis coach and director of Tennis Fitness Phsyio, a Queensland based company specialising in sports medicine, elite tennis player development, strength and conditioning, and childhood motor learning programmes.

Ulrik Larsen BThpy MAPA is an Australian Physiotherapy Association sports physiotherapist with a special interest in clinical Pilates. He is physiotherapist to Queensland Academy of Sport men's water polo team.

Chris Mallac is head physiotherapist at the Queensland Reds Super 14 Rugby and former head of sports medicine at Bath Rugby in England.

Notes

Notes

Notes